CANALS
OF FRANCE

CANALS
OF FRANCE

MICHEL-PAUL SIMON

ÉDITIONS DU CHÊNE

THE CANALS OF FRANCE

— Navigable rivers
— Working canals
— Canals being or projected to be rehabilitated
— Non-navigable rivers

0   50   100 km

Dunkerque
Fontinettes
(Ascenseur)
Saint-Omer
Lille
Abbeville
Sambre
Oise
Le Havre
Rouen
Aisne
Compiègne
Reims
Verdun
Metz
Caen
Orne
Seine
Oise
The Canal
Saint-Denis
The Ourcq
Canal
Meaux
Aisne
Meuse
Moselle
Nancy
Rhine
Canal
Strasbourg
Marne-
Rhine
Rhin
Saint-Malo
The Ille and
Rance Canal
PARIS
The Canal
Saint-Martin
Aube
Ill
Brest
The
Nantes-Brest
Mayenne
Mayenne
Saint-Mammès
The Loing
Canal
Montereau
Aube
Marne
Épinal
Colmar
Pontivy
Rohan
Rennes
Le Mans
The
Orleans
Canal
Montargis
The Burgundy
Tanlay
Moselle
Mulhouse
La Gacilly
The Blavet
Canal
Sarthe
Orléans
The Briare
Canal
Ancy-le-Franc
Belfort
Besançon
Lorient
Redon
Vilaine
Loir
The Nivernais
Canal
Canal
Saône
The Rhone-Rhine Canal
Angers
Loire
The Sauldre
Canal
Briare
Dijon
Nantes
Loire
Beuvron
Sauldre
Chitry-
les-Mines
Corbigny
The Doubs
Vienne
Vierzon
Cher
The Berry
Canal
Sardy
Pouilly-
en-Auxois
Chalon-
sur-Saône
Indre
Bourges
Fontblisse
Autize
Niortaise
Creuse
Montluçon
Allier
Roanne
Sèvre
Mignon
Niort
Vienne
Loire
Lyon
Charente
Angoulême
Isère
Périgueux
Vézère
Dordogne
Valence
Bordeaux
Dordogne
Isle
Bergerac
The Lalinde
Canal
Lot
Rhône
Lot
Cahors
Durance
Nérac
Adour
Baise
Montauban
Avignon
Condom
Tarn
Beaucaire
Gave de Pau
Toulouse
The
Canal
du
Midi
Sète
Marseille
Bidouze
Garonne
Carcassonne
Narbonne

4

CONTENTS

THE WORLD OF CANALS

FONTAINE-les-CLERS. - Les Écluses

Less than a century ago, geography lessons for French children in primary schools included a topic that is no longer part of the school curriculum: the navigable waterways. The teacher hung a map on the board showing France criss-crossed by a multitude of blue and green veins. It was to be studied, just as the map of the national motorways and the map of the railways were. Pointing out the principal axes, the teacher explained that these fluvial routes spanned more than twelve thousand kilometres and were admired throughout Europe, if not the world. The teacher then went on to explain the difference between a lateral canal and a junction canal. The pupils generally looked bored during this exposé, but grew excited as soon as the railways map was brought out. The newspapers at the time were filled with railway exploits, particularly those concerning the BB electric locomotive. Their excitement reached a peak when the teacher drew their attention to the map of the national motorways. Everyone was talking about how the new Citroen could get you from Paris to Marseille in a single day.

Novelty always wears off, however. These children are now parents and grandparents. Their "thrill thresholds" have been raised higher and higher by the numerous technological advances of their times, such as the Mistral train, the Corail, the turbotrain and the TGV. The railway company is now associated with strikes and budget deficits. The thrill of the motorways has faded as well, leaving a bitter aftertaste of accidents and traffic jams. The beautiful tree-lined roadways are no longer part of the collective conscious. Some say disillusion always rises whenever a century is winding down towards a new one.

LEFT-HAND PAGE
In many regions, the canal-diggers created the French countryside.

ABOVE
A landscape where the barge is the centre of attention.

Let's come back to the map of the free-flowing waterways. The network is still in existence, yet more and more pleasure boats now ply the waters. They are manned by families, smiling radiantly or wearing the solemn expressions of great navigators. Their boats are fitted out as veritable vacation flats. People tend to slow down as they cross over a bridge and watch them drift by. Occasionally, they follow them a bit if the road permits and catch up with them at the lock. The lock-keeper slowly hurries out of the gatehouse, gives a good turn of the crank on one side, then the other. The water levels come equal. One father, in somewhat confusing terms, explains to his children what is happening and how the locks work. The lock-keeper and the captain thank each other with an amicable wave, and the boat leaves. The lock-keeper ambles towards the gatehouse once again. For an instant, as she faces the onlookers, it almost looks like she is about to take a bow, like an actress at the end of a show.

You almost have the impression you've seen something really rare, a sort of secret rite coming from the depths of all time. Where was the boat coming from, so far from the sea? Where is it going? The slow movements, the gentleness of the green environment around the river .... and this mysterious gate with its muted sounds of water lapping against its wet, mossy walls are nearly hypnotic.

We thus discover, in this third millenium, that the waterways are still pursuing their discreet existence – that of a whole other world of which we were hardly even aware. They are like a historical monument which covers practically all of the French territory.

The navigable waterways are no longer twelve thousand, but eight hundred, kilometres long. The network is double; it is composed of a few canals with extra-large beds and of improved rivers adapted to ultramodern craft. A single pushed

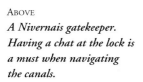

ABOVE
A Nivernais gatekeeper. Having a chat at the lock is a must when navigating the canals.

barge can easily carry the load of one hundred trucks. In addition to these rare liquid motorways, there is also a multitude of little loops of canals dating from the times of the Kings. Barges have disappeared from these smaller routes because they became too large for them over time. The canals are adorable, sometimes minuscule, and are lined with dollhouse gates. They wind through the country and feature an assortment of canal bridges, tunnels, boat elevators, and liquid intersections – all grandiose in style and brilliantly engineered.

The single-motor barge: quiet and trustworthy, it transports as much merchandise as ten big lorries with the fuel consumption of just one.

France is like a mountain, with rivers and streams radiating out in all directions – the perfect topography for inland navigation. Canals easily connect the various rivers. The construction and use of the canals, and of the waterways in general, has been highly beneficial both in terms of transporting goods and facilitating travel. Even the most modest of vessels represents a minimum of ten or twelve wagons. A single man could operate one year round, except during periods of heavy freeze. Carriages, in contrast, required a lot of man- and animal-power to transport them and could not proceed in snow or mud. Water travel thus constituted a great advantage for those regions hindered by geographical constraints.

It was then discovered that if there was a way to get enough water to the upper – the highest – section of the reach, the water could be made not only to descend the length of a valley, but also to flow in an entirely different direction. This opened the way for the creation of artificial canals, which allowed waterways to cross mountains, and thus replace land crossings. It became possible to go from one basin to another, over hundreds of kilometres. The canalization of Europe came to be and gave birth to a network of waterways that enables travel from Bordeaux to Basel, from Marseille to Hamburg, or from Paris to Berlin – by boat.

The collecting reach was the great invention of a Renaissance engineer, Adam de Craponne, who discovered the way to detour streams and bring them together to form lakes. The invention was first applied to the connection between the Loire and the Seine rivers, begun under the reign of Henri IV. The "seven locks" of Rogny, which although no longer in service are still in place, bear witness

The stonework on the side of this hill doesn't look like much. However, it is what permitted the first boat to pass from the Loire to the Seine in 1610 at Rogny-les-Sept-Écluses.

to this historical construction. At the time of its greatest extension (around 1910), the network connected small and medium-sized cities all across France. Most have completely forgotten their fluvial origins: Périgueux, Troyes, Decazeville, Albi, Tours, Vierzon, Orléans, Belfort, and others. Some hadn't seen a boat in years until the recent advent of pleasure boating; among them, Angoulême, Cahors, Epinal, Roanne, Le Mans, Dijon, Rennes, Niort, and Laval.

Once a canal is up and running, its efficiency is astounding. The great triangular trade is just one example. From Nantes, low-value goods were sent to Africa in exchange for slaves. These slaves were sold in the West Indies, and the vessels returned to France loaded down with rum and sugar. This configuration could not have functioned without a fourth "side" to the triangle – the rivers and canals. The low-value goods sent to Africa were fabrics and tools manufactured by factories along the waterways; they arrived at the seaports via the canals before being shipped to Africa. The goods from the colonies arriving in exchange would never have been distributed without these canals.

In 1810, the French had not fallen victim to famine, largely due to inland navigation. This allowed for the massive transport of supplies, and widespread food shortages which could previously have been caused by regional shortages, were no longer a threat. When necessary, the barges travelled by night in convoys using navigation lanterns. This expanded service has often been in use throughout history, for the last time during the critical period of 1940-1945.

By the end of the 19th century, the canal system was made up of waterways of various sizes – much like the railway system. The smallest craft were used so that even the narrowest waterways could be navigated. These economic constraints were surmounted by the energetic renovation plan of Charles de Freycinet, a minister of the Third Republic who standardized the sizes of all railways and waterways. Although De Freycinet has been largely forgotten by the railways, his memory is still alive and well in the boating world: he left behind him a certain type of boat, generally referred to as the barge. Administratively speaking, it is a "self-propelled barge"; for the sailor, it is a *freycinet*. The barge was inspired by a sea-going type of vessel characteristic of the north of France. Since De Freycinet's time, the barge measures thirty-eight and one-half metres in length and five metres in width. Perfectly adapted to the normalized lock-gates, the Freycinet barge became popular throughout Europe. It was even responsible for the disappearance of many other regional vessels, some of which had descended from Gallo-Roman designs. Barges were first made of wood, later of steel; they were initially towed by horses, but later equipped with a large diesel motor after a short intermediary phase of being towed by tractor. A couple could easily live on the barge, albeit in rather cramped quarters, and this gave rise to "long haul" exploitation. Around 1900, the sailor and his wife became eternal travellers coasting along the twelve thousand kilometres of the network night and day. The waterways also transformed these sailors into drifters; they had no fixed address, they were mobile. They lived on their constantly-moving worksite, which allowed them to choose their clients and their cargo in the free freight exchange system of the time. They owned their boats, which were also their homes, their roots and their culture. In reality, they were Kings in their own little Kingdoms – anomalies in modern society – and were often likened to gypsies because of their festive way of life and their bizarre vocabulary, and they were somewhat touchy where their honour was concerned.

In addition to being a form of low-cost transportation, the single motor is also the home of its owner. Means of transportation, home, business capital... it is indeed unique in our modern times.

This tribe, however, slowly died out, as did the *freycinet* which could be seen coming around the bend of a canal, loaded with merchandise. They were slow, but they transported heavy cargoes at unbeatable prices. The sight of the passing barge – laundry blowing in the wind and children frolicking on the deck as the father manned the helm for his twelve-hour day – became more and more rare as time went on. It was being replaced by more modern vessels on cemented rivers: convoys of souped-up barges, river and sea-going transporters, two-ton oil tankers, and others. The smaller canals which snaked through the countryside in their shallow beds, reaching only smaller, far-away places, were saved from sure death by the new interest for pleasure boating which developed in the 1960's. These small canals were fiercely defended by this movement, as we will see in the coming pages. What urban planner today would dare propose to fill up one of these canals to build an in-road? The re-opening of a clogged canal to create a lake or pond is more common these days.

There are many different ways to discover the canals: at the helm, of course, for those who own or have rented a boat. This form of vacation is rapidly becoming a classic, as is being a passenger on a barge-hotel for those who wish to avoid the modest worries of navigating their own vessel. Newcomers often experience a strange feeling at first. They are seeing France, and yet discovering a side of the country previously unknown to them. They are outside of the France they know, and yet are in the very heart of it – in the wings of the French stage. There are no cars, no asphalt, no shops; instead, there are gardens, roofs jutting out of the greenery. What was that castle? What are these noises? A rooster's crow, the bells of a convent, the gurgling of a washtub. These are the sounds he hears, punctuated from time to time by the sounds of water cascading through a lockgate. You don't miss much from the water, especially not the rise and fall of the earth around you. Boats, like bicycles, emphasize differences in levels, for they are both resolutely horizontal travellers.

Another somewhat troubling aspect of river navigation is its association of opposites: the boat and its antithesis, the countryside. The ambiance is incontestably a nautical one. The low snoring of the motor, the red buoy, and the stowed anchor are proof of this. Yet, the ambiance is one of country as well, with the banks only a few metres away where a flock of animals has stopped to drink.

Yet, there is a strange symmetry. You find yourself in a mirror: the semicircle of a

bridge becomes a full circle when reflected in the water. You sail straight through the heart of the target. The trees, too, are all double! When the treetops come together above your head, they also come together at your feet. It's a strange kind of surrealism, as if you were in the midst of a film by Jean Cocteau.

And then there's the gentle euphoria of canal navigation. After a few days on the water, you fall into a sort of enchanted state. It is sometimes monotonous, and this monotony only reinforces the dream-like peacefulness of it all. You can also discover the canals by bicycle, on foot, or by horse along the towpaths. You sometimes make better time than the boats themselves do. A canal is a time-machine that plunges you back into the past. You travel at the speed of a walking horse, slower than a bicycle. You count in days, not in kilometres. The locks all bear dates, generally old ones. Some gate mechanisms have been in service for over a century. How many mechanical devices do we know – be it a sewing machine or a funicular – that have been operating day after day for decades? Where else can you still see drawbridges that actually work?

Canals are totally artificial landscapes. Ironically, they are wrought by the hands of man, and yet they appear so natural. They organize nature, and thereby streamline its force. Harnessed water imposes agricultural order for its sedentary

Pleasure boats are becoming more common than barges on those canals.

13

Between Lutzelbourg and Arzviller, one of the gates coming in from the Vosges Mountains. It takes you down into the Alsatian Plain.

and enterprising inhabitants; linear plantations along the canal attest to this, at least those which haven't disappeared. They are like a code for those who can decipher it. On the Midi Canal in the south of France, cypress trees are a harbinger of a lock. In other parts of France, there are fruit trees instead of cypress trees. A double row of poplars mark the passage of the Ourcq Canal on the Briard plateau. Trees break the winter winds, give shade in the summer, and provide wood for the owner, who distributes it to riverside residents or employees according to very precise rules. On the Burgundy Canal in autumn, walnuts fall from the sky and are collected by passersby. This is the order of the world of canals.

Art in general shapes the character of a landscape. The gatehouses are like so many reference points of centuries past. Stones, bricks and even the cement used for the gate (of the only network signed by Le Corbusier) comes from the past. Everything comes from the earth, including the iron side rails. An old canal is forever a monument to princely glory, and its image must be a powerful one. The obelisks and bas-reliefs are there to proclaim the reign of human order and the savoir-faire of the Department of Civil Engineering (which rarely missed a chance to toot its own horn via these waterway creations). Any structure or major technical innovation devoid of these flourishes indicates that the budget came up short. A triumphal arch had surely been part of the original layout.

Finally, a canal can be seen as a hydraulic machine, spread out over hundreds of kilometres, its organs and levels adjusted with admirable precision. Geometry in the truest sense of the word – the measurement of the land – takes on its full meaning. You can just imagine the engineers of the past – accompanied by their clerks in heavy carriages, on horseback or on a mule, escorted by a local guide – criss-crossing the region in all kinds of weather, perhaps camping out when the inn was full. They were plotting the terrain and drawing up its contours. Their plans represented leagues and leagues of land which they covered tens of times before having reconnoitred the territory and weighed the practical difficulties. How many working men were available in the parish? What was the flow-rate of the stream? For a league of canal, he had to dig so many channels in order to get the water necessary to fill it. All this remains invisible to the eyes of navigators and visitors. Nevertheless, these mini-canals constitute hundreds of kilometres of water, flowing out of springs or lakes sometimes quite removed from the canal they were to feed. Five of them flow into the Burgundy Canal, five ponds which have flooded the vales of the region. Fishermen, fooled by their appearance, still believe they are fully natural. There are four of them in the Langres region which feed into the Marne-Saône Canal, where the inhabitants have set up nautical clubs and pisciculture basins. There are many examples. These "feeders" are the most secret components of the immense hydraulic machine. Others include the pumps operating off the waterflow like watermills. They raise water tens of metres higher before letting it fall by landings at the desired speed. An excellent example is the one on the Marne for the Ourcq Canal. On long-distance trips, there were so many obstacles that had to be drilled through or skirted while ensuring that water levels were continually adjusted fromone river to the next.

ABOVE
The aqueduct of Montreuillon. It is impossible to guess that this viaduct is actually an aqueduct. It is twenty kilometres long and carries water to the Nivernais Canal.

BELOW
The Dordogne River at Trémolat.

THE LOCK:

A MASTERPIECE OF SOFT TECHNOLOGY

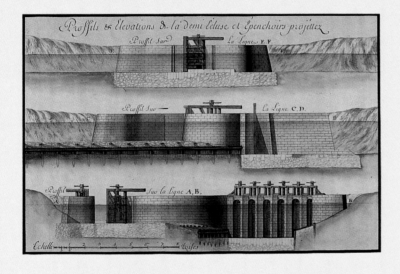

Since the Renaissance, engineers have been drawing up plans for the canals. It is a wonderful thing to see them again today.

Contrary to popular legend, the modern-day lock didn't just spring from Leonardo da Vinci's imagination. In reality, it was the result of a long, time-consuming process of evolution. In summer, water was in short supply and river-folk naturally had the idea of damming up the river. Upstream, the water level rose. They soon discovered that they could build several dams, transforming the river into a series of pseudo-lakes. The problem remained that boats could not pass from one "lake" to another.

Later on, they added an opening to the dam, which could be used to let a boat through it. However, this system was impractical and quite dangerous, as it provoked artificial floods. They called this opening a gate, a sluice, a bargeman's door. You can still see a few of them on the Loir, where they aren't used to pass boats anymore but rather to regulate the water flow. They are operated by an appointed river-dweller. The Romans were already using this set-up long ago, calling it a *cataracta*. It is the opposite of a dam, because in normal times the water flowed naturally to keep the mills in action. They closed the passage temporarily every time a boat needed to pass, in order to accumulate sufficient water. The Middle Ages saw no improvement of this system.

The last stage in the evolution process was fundamental: in reaction to the abrupt, dangerous nature of passages through the dams, a second dam was built with another gate placed two or three hundred metres downstream. The water released by the upstream gate carried the boat gently until it stopped at the second gate. They then opened the second one. The "two-step passage" had been created. In between these two dams, the banks were dug out to increase the mass of reserve waters which constituted an oval basin allowing several boats to wait for the opening. This double gate is the direct ancestor of our modern-day water-locks, according to Charles Berg, a historical researcher. Many of these old sluice-dams still exist in France, long-abandoned yet still perfectly recognizable. For example, there is the one on the Thouet, a sub-tributary of the Loire, or again, the one on the Ae, a tributary of the Lys. Leonardo da Vinci had already seen this system successfully applied during a visit to the Naviglio Grande in Piedmont. During a visit to France, Da Vinci stood before the sluices on the Cher and studied their operation. He began to wonder what would happen if the intermediary body of water were reduced to the size just larger than that of a boat. The advantages of such a system would be the reduction of water consumption, and increased levels of security and ease in the manoeuvre. With a minimum of masonry, you would get a maximum of flow. The first gate of this sort was built near Vierzon, as revealed by the vestiges discovered during an excavation in 1923 on the Yèvre River. Ten lock-gate foundations were uncovered during dredging, each one presented as "da Vinci's Gate" or as "the oldest one in France", if not the world.

With the development of the locks, which often follow one after another in a series, it became possible to take a waterway down a steep incline along stairways or ladders of calm water. A lock is a masterpiece of soft technology: Using materials as simple as stones for the holding tanks, wood for the doors, and a little iron

Thanks to the Brittany Canal network, you can go from Nantes to Brest in a boat and never touch saltwater.

for the hinges, tons and tons of merchandise could be ferried upstream to remote areas, from the mouth of a river towards its source. What effort was involved? The simple turning of the cranks at each gate, which even a child could do. Energy consumption: zero. Damages caused: zero. Day after day, lock-keepers across France lifted some three hundred tons of water a distance of several metres by simple opening and closing sluices. It is the water that does all the work!

MUNICIPAL WATERS

THE CANALS OF PARIS

You can be sure that Parisian drivers feel somewhat frustrated whenever the Crimée Bridge is raised, and the route is blocked to let boats pass through the canal below. The modern population is thus reminded of the otherwise "invisible" canal system, which dates back to long ago, and is still extremely useful. The canals make Paris an even more beautiful city, and were at the root of its creation. Yet virtually none of the fishermen who cast their lines into the canals, and pedestrians who stroll along their shores, and painters who find inspiration in them, are capable of explaining where the water comes from or where it goes. This may be an homage to those who built the canals: So harmonious is their design, so perfect their integration into the surrounding environment, no one would ever think to question their presence. The Paris Canals appear to be a simple work of nature, like a river or a mountain.

The canals of Paris – the Ourcq, the Saint-Martin, and the Saint-Denis – owe their existence to the fear of hunger. As any King knows, hungry people spell trouble. Only the waterways could permit the massive transport of foodstuffs and other materials necessary for the growth of such a big city. Paris, in fact, is a river site, and Parisian residents of olden days were well aware of this. It was an important centre of fluvial trading and shipping. There have always been two distinct components to this activity: the upstream area and the downstream area, each with its specific characteristics and functions. The "breaking point" for these two areas is the bottleneck created by a string of three (today only two) islands, which produce a zone with heavier currents. The currents caused those going downriver to stop, and

LEFT
The canals of Paris have been made even more attractive: here, the Villette Basin.

NEXT DOUBLE-PAGE
At the Sevran lock, you leave the Parisian suburbs and penetrate into the green, touristic area of the Ourcq Canal.

The existing Ourcq canal starts in the garden of this beautiful 18th-century estate. Port-aux-Perches is located more than a hundred kilometres from Paris and yet is still in the Parisian region.

kept those travelling upstream from continuing their route. This inevitably gave rise to the creation of warehouses and surveillance authorities. From upstream came low-value goods such as wood, fodder, Burgundy wines, and stones from Champagne for building fortifications. The route for those travelling upstream was much more difficult and expensive, creating extra costs for towing. The products were of greater specific value: meat, cheese, fruit, and vegetables from Normandy, fabrics from Rouen, and other exotic products. Had the contrary been the case, the system wouldn't have worked – and Lutetia simply would never have become the equivalent of Paris!

We need to consider the geographical and hydraulic aspects of this situation in order to understand how the city we know today came to be. It was not the result of sheer human will. The critical point is a large bend in the Seine River. The Right Bank had a swifter current, which resulted in a deeper, more clear-cut shore. This is where large vessels could moor, and men and cargoes could disembark. Consequently, land was more expensive and more money was concentrated on the Right Bank. It came to be a power centre concentrating the merchandise that needed to be guarded and eventually taxed: Palais Royal and the Hôtel de Ville appeared and, with them, the first Counts and Provosts. The Louvre couldn't have been built anywhere else. The situation was different on the Left Bank. The current there was weak, and the banks easily flooded and difficult to access. Small economic value meant a smaller population. The monks built their abbeys there, far from the busy centre and close to the then-vast agricultural terrains. In addition to the abbeys, the Jardin des Plantes, the Sorbonne, the Académie Française, the Observatoire, and other centres of learning were developed. The Seine River thus provides the key to the current lay-out of the entire city, not only the North-South axis, but also that of the East-West. Industries were established in the east because vessels unloaded their merchandise there, outside the city limits and the toll zones. Navigation is also easier there. The neighbourhoods in the west were in great demand because they were quiet and spacious. Large companies set up their headquarters, close to the affluence of the well-to-do Parisians.

Some historians maintain that Paris became the capital of the Kingdom as a result of the feudal wars, and that other cities such as Senlis or Provins, which were more important at certain times, had equal reason to become capitals. These historians

have unfortunately neglected the importance of waterways in their theories. France's capital could have been Soissons, Compiègne, Amiens, Conflans-Sainte-Honorine, Lyon, or even Tours; all had waterways. But in no way could Senlis or Provins ever have filled the role: They simply did not have the liquid means to grow and expand.

Ensuring that a sufficient quantity of foodstuffs reached the capital each day was the somewhat prosaic worry of the monarch – if he wanted to keep the crown on his head. As a result, the rivers of the Ile-de-France region – the Ourcq, the Bièvre, the Vanne, the Yvette, and the Morin – received a great deal of attention early on, as they permitted the transport of fresh market produce from surrounding villages. This is confirmed in texts dating back to François I. Between 1529 and 1636, the Ourcq was equipped with sluices all the way to its confluence with the Marne, thus providing a source of safe, regular navigation. Modernization of the canals was an on-going process, largely due to the constant requests of the wood and cereal merchants. From time to time, a minister would commission his best engineers to study a project which surfaced time and time again: detouring the Ourcq River so that it flowed into Paris.

ABOVE
The gate at Ferté-Milon has seen a lot of vessels cross through, like these turn-of-the-century flutes.

Eventually, the project was undertaken. The Ourcq, whose source is more than thirty leagues (one hundred twenty kilometres) from Paris, would spill into a basin near the Faubourg Saint-Antoine (at the Place de la Nation). At this time, the Ourcq was designated to be a polyvalent waterway: it should "carry boats, supply water for new fountains, contribute to the beauty of public parks, and implement factories' activities". The confluence of the Ourcq and the Marne, situated at Lizy, was to change faces many times. The Ourcq has been split up, reshaped, circuited, and intersected by all sorts of archaic models of locks to such an extent that there have been serious doubts about its true course. River archflology has become a science in its own right, and the Ourcq is an ideal terrain for research. One scholar, Jacques de la Garde, recently revealed that some areas had seen three different canals, each leaving its trace of small works of art or filled-up passages – like so many legacies.

The French Revolution came and went, the Consulate followed, and then came the Empire. The Ourcq entered the national domain. -"What do the Parisians want?" asked Napoleon, somewhat anxious at the beginning of his reign.

-"Water, sire," responded the minister Chaptal.

-"Water. Let it flow to their fountains."

It was easy enough to fetch water from the corner of the street instead of paying a sou (5 centimes) per fifteen litres. The First Consul examined a series of different projects and, on 29 Floréal of Year X, he signed a decree. The plan strongly resembled

RIGHT-HAND PAGE
The Fresnes lock on the Ourcq canal.

BELOW
The boat is king; the bridge raises up automatically at its approach and the cars wait. Near Claye-Souilly.

a battle order and commanded that the Ourcq River be "brought to Paris and emptied into a basin near La Villette, detoured by a derivation canal coming from the Seine just under the basin of the Arsenal". The force and speed of these decisions was astounding. The founding decree was dated May 19, 1802. The landowner problem, a worry for all developers today, was quickly dismissed: "The terrain will be acquired by mutual agreement or by the decision of experts." On August 13, an order was published outlining the project: it was to be financed by a levy on the Parisian city toll, owned by the Prefect of the Seine, directed by the Department of Civil Engineering, and launched on September 23 of the same year – just five weeks after the initial decision. On September 15, the hydraulic engineer Pierre-Simon Gérard was chosen to oversee the work. He had already accompanied Bonaparte to Egypt and seen the ancient Red Sea canal. Prussian prisoners represented free manpower, and fifteen batallions of four hundred men each were put to work digging the canals. Napoleon also put convicts at the disposition of the contractors, who nevertheless had to furnish "shovels, picks and wheelbarrows, as well as meals". Peasants not labouring their fields at the time came to Paris to work and earn some extra money.

The job was completed in six years. The new waterway began at the Port-aux-Perches near Ferté-Milon, in the Aisne region. It was part of the Ourcq River until its confluence with the Marne, then followed the hillside artificially. At several points, one could see the Marne down below as the canal skirted the town of Meaux. It then

LIZY-sur-OURCQ – Le Port du Canal

Edit., Soyer

OPPOSITE
The canal irrigates the economy along its way. Here, the Lizy sawmill circa 1900.

NEXT DOUBLE-PAGE
The building on the right dates from the last century. It's an old warehouse. This sort of «general store» reminds us of the original activities of the Villette basin. Nearby, its twin was burned down a few years ago.

27

spilled into a pretty basin in the village of La Villette, situated just before the Porte de Pantin toll barrier. The basin was decorated by the architect Nicolas Ledoux in the same neoclassical style as the toll rotunda. It was a magnificent mirror of water, seven hundred metres round surrounded by four rows of trees forming a triumphant lane – the liquid equivalent of the Champs-Elysées. The water left the basin on its right-hand side, flowing through a circular aqueduct to Parisian fountains at the rate of three hundred thousand cubic metres per day. On the left, a symmetrical sluice gate dammed up the water. It later became the Canal Saint-Martin. The site was an immediate success. Little waterside cafés known as guinguettes sprang up all around the basin. Parisians came in great numbers to stroll about, and the first great freeze in winter saw the basin transformed into a giant ice-skating rink. In summer, swimming and skiff competitions were held. Under the Restoration, it was one of the most fashionable places in all of Paris. Official ceremonies and parades were held at La Villette. The armies of the Tsar, of Prussia, and of Austria marched in pomp and circumstance around the basin. It was the fashionable place to stage shows and celebrations.

The circular out-flowing aqueduct later became the Canal Saint-Denis. It crossed the northern part of the city on its way to the Seine (it was supposed to spill into the Seine), at Conflans-Sainte-Honorine. This never happened. There just weren't enough other sources of water to feed it along the way. In the end, it had to

BELOW

The moving bridge on Crimée Street still functions with the pressure of the water itself - no other fuel is required. A bit of modernism has been added with the installation of a radar that detects the boat and starts the gate moving.

join the Seine further up, at Gennevilliers. Opened to water travel in 1821, the canal was a precious time-saver, avoiding the interminable meanders with their inevitable islands, fishing installations, and other time-consuming obstacles. Inland water navigation was most conveniently developed along the route to Normandy, but most importantly, merchandise from the seaport Le Havre was shipped to Paris.

The third section of the Parisian canal network is the Canal Saint-Martin. La Villette basin is twenty-six metres lower than the Seine, and the Seine is just four thousand five hundred metres to the south. In between the two was a fairly tightly woven urban development. The land was expensive and the terrain quite unfavourable, the substratum being composed of gypsum and thus highly water-soluble. In order to acquire the land, the government expropriated more than a thousand landowners. Mastery of the ground was achieved by a multitude of artificial beds, bridges, and even some arched passages. Despite all these difficulties, the canal was finished in less than four years. It arrived at the Bastille in the old trench, forming a basin of nearly six hundred metres, and immediately grew into an important boating area. The Isle of Louvier – Paris's third island, then covered with stacks of wood as high as some of the buildings – would later be united with the bank by filling in the arm which today supports the boulevard Morland. In terms of the Parisians' water supply, it was a. mission accomplished In less than twenty years, life was completely transformed by free, pure water flowing from the one thousand eight hundred municipal fountains. Houses with running water soon became commonplace, and the two thousand water-boys had to be recycled into other professions. The Prefect Rambuteau proclaimed his great satisfaction: "Who would have believed that Parisians had barely eight litres of drinking water per head. Today, they have a hundred!"

Commercial traffic is still active in the heart of Paris and is even growing - especially every time there is major urban construction underway. This was the case for the Stadium of France in Saint-Denis. The barges spare the city the coming and going of hundreds of trucks.

That is how the network of the Paris Canals came to be. It is made up of over one hundred thirty kilometres of waterways which, exceptionally, belong to the community and not to the State.

Navigation was totally revolutionized: It took two days less to get to Rouen, and sailing from the Quai de la Rapée to the Isle of Saint-Denis required only eight hours instead of three days. Storehouses were built at La Villette to keep wheat dry

and protect stocks from thieves. Today, you can still see one of these warehouses, which has been converted into an artists' atelier. This area soon became the most important industrial centre of Paris. Along the Ourcq Canal sailed the slim store ships of the time *(flûtes)*, which were guided by poles. The canal's downstream current – the equivalent of half the speed of a person walking – made the guide-poles a necessity. Travelling upstream, they were towed either by a mule or by two men. The *flûtes*, made of iron instead of wood, were twenty-eight metres long by three metres wide. They were especially designed for this waterway, following the specifications established by the decree of 1840. There are still a few around today. They are used by the Canal Services of Paris. These store ships carried seventy tons. There were also half-sizes, which were easier to operate. This regional river traffic filled a vitally important function of rivers at the time: that of local service. The inhabitants of the area were very attached to it, and the service continued right up into the 1960s. "I remember," says a retired man form Meaux, "that the Samaritaine department store delivered my bedroom set by boat when I got married." *Les Bateaux Fournier* (Fournier Boating Co.) is still present in the memories of inhabitants today. The transport of passengers by boat competed fairly with the Meaux stage-coach at the time, but declined with the advent of the train. Mail was also distributed by boat. For more than twenty years, from 1837 to 1860, travellers could take "highspeed" boats, towed by three horses at a trot, travelling as fast as the train. These boats were very long and narrow, measuring twenty-two metres in length and only two metres in width. Built out of acacia wood, they skimmed through the waters at a fast clip. They had priority over all other vessels on the canal and let everybody know it with their strident blows of the horn. A rider preceded them, opening the locks so they wouldn't lose a second of their precious time. They had a special first-class area, with a heated salon in winter.

FOLLOWING DOUBLE-PAGE
On each side of the Napoleon Canal, Paris of the 3rd millennium.

RIGHT-HAND PAGE
The Nicolas Ledoux Rotunda, the gate called the "Fermiers Généraux" where taxes were collected its back side was originally a toll gate. It was recently restored and completes this grand avenue of water on the Place Stalingrad. In the forefront, a stop-over place for pleasure boaters.

OPPOSITE
A unique thing in the history of French transports: a boat being towed at a brisk trot in order to compete with the railway.

The Ourcq also saw the birth of a unique set-up in France: the boat-transporter using a hydraulic elevator in Beauval. Near Meaux, the canal passes as close as five hundred metres from the Marne River. But in order to pass from one to the other, you had to go all the way to Paris and come up the other side: a distance of over one hundred kilometres. The very dynamic Fournier Boating Company decided to build an enormous gutter between the two, which it used to transfer its own boats from one to the other. It was operated by a sort of trolley run by cables and "fuelled" by the movement of the waterfall itself. On each side of the trolley, a basin was installed to catch the boat as it landed in the water. Today, there is no trace of Beauval's ingenious transfer system, except for a few remnants rusting on private property. The original plans are part of France's national archives, and the Canal Service has plans to re-create the same type of machine. It will be electronically operated and used to transfer tourist and pleasure vessels from the Ourcq Canal to the Marne River.

In the underground. The light-wells come from flowered hills on what is the Boulevard Richard-Lenoir for those above.

The one hundred kilometres of intensely green banks surrounding the canal make for a beautiful landscape, despite the poorly-developed urban areas. One comes upon rest areas for yachtsmen, modernized yet not disfigured locks, and art works open to the public. The most representative of these is the water elevation plant at Trilbardou, whose enormous "Sagebien" paddle-wheel lifts the waters of the Marne River to feed the canal. It turns five hundred times per

Yesterday and today (left-hand page) water transport contrasts its quiet efficiency with the frenzy of Parisian automobile traffic.

235. PARIS — Canal Saint-Martin - Pont Tournant   C. L. C.

Those who hang around never miss the spectacle of the lock gates' operation. The locks and the footbridges of the Canal Saint-Martin are part of this tradition, as is the facade of the Hotel du Nord, a classified Historical Monument.

minute and has been doing so for one hundred and forty years. Here, you come across amateur sailors thrilled at the pleasure of spending the night in a place which is so close to Paris, yet so peaceful. It is a place where nature is undisturbed and host to the likes of rabbits, squirrels, kingfishers, and even weasels. Canoeists also abound, and the paddlers speak grandly of this prodigious space of freedom. The small size of the canoes allows them to cruise freely from the Marne to the old river, travelling upstream on the tiny routes. These relatively unknown waterways belong to the city of Paris and are as beautiful as their names: the Clignon, the Thérouanne, the Beuvronne, the Grivette, and the Gergogne – like names from a medieval tale! You also see lots of people travelling on rented pénichettes (houseboats) or again, sight-seeing boats full of tourists – the *Pierre-Simon Gérard* being an excellent example. The Ourcq Canal is more beautiful and clean today than it ever was before.

After experiencing such peace and beauty, it is somewhat startling to enter the capital and suddenly find yourself face-to-face with 21st-century Paris: the ultra-modern Géode at La Villette, the Cité des Sciences, the green expanses of grass, and small lakes dotted with spindly newsstands. The festive spirit of La Villette of past times lives on: the little theatres and small gazebo-like structures with their light structures remind one of parties and romantic meetings of another period. On the

right, you see the intersection of the canals, where industrial barges laboriously make their way up the Saint-Denis Canal. It's a vision of modern inland water transport, indeed far from the old barges. Each is loaded down with construction materials equal to that carried by ten, twenty, or even thirty lorries. These enormous barges silently make their way along the Grand Stade (grand stadium) without proclaiming their principal quality: the extraordinary economy of their services. Barge transport costs about six centimes per ton per kilometre – an unheard-of low price! They travel towards the east, and won't be followed by yachts or other pleasure vessels; the Saint-Denis Canal isn't particularly attractive. However, the basin of La Villette, which has been undergoing renovation for the last few years, is indeed beautiful. It has again become similar to how it was depicted in engravings from the Restoration period. The Nicolas Ledoux rotunda has been restored and fitted with new columns. It is charming by day, grandiose by night. On the following section of the Saint-Martin Canal, little brick houses and cast-iron fittings take us back to the beginning of the 19th century filled with Parisian folklore. Fishermen line the banks, policemen stroll the grounds, and vegetable stands dot the perimeters. The footbridges constitute an ideal backdrop to the scene, and you find yourself uttering "Atmosphere, Atmosphere", those legendary words from Marcel Carné's film, when passing near the Hôtel du Nord.

The Basin of the Arsenal whose gate opens into the Seine, is the pleasure port of Paris. River navigators come from as far as Basel, Amsterdam or Toulouse. Just as in the old days, it is still an important meeting place for all kinds of vessels and accents.

Further south, you come across the boulevard Richard-Lenoir with its enigmatic masses of flowers planted around equally mysterious copings. These sorts of wells were built over the canal on its way to the Arsenal. The dull blue-green light filtering from them to the canal below is both soothing and peaceful. The canal was open when first built, then covered over during the period of Haussmanian urban development. It took four years to dig out the Saint-Martin Canal and forty years to cover just a part of it! The work was finished in 1907. Continuing south, you come to a point where a multitude of important historical periods meet: the Bastille ditch, the July Column, and the ossuary of the Commune. When waiting for the underground at the Bastille station, you have a splendid view of the Arsenal Basin to the south. It has become a nice yachting port in a lovely garden inaugurated in 1983. Old postcards show this site when it was a meeting place for regional boating operations where money, merchandise, and news were exchanged. Old legends speak of the nocturnal activities of this disreputable spot – the diverse depredations and plundering, dagger fights, drinking, abusing the ladies, and other unsavoury things ...

THE LAST BARGEMAN

THE LALINDE CANAL

The Dordogne River is truly magnificent. It provided invaluable transport for centuries and boosted the prosperity of the region, from the Auvergne basin to Bordeaux. It carried argentats and courpets, wooden transport vessels named after the cities where they were built. They often rested on the banks, waiting until the waters were "open for business", that is, high enough to carry them. Upon arrival, these disposable vessels were unloaded (they generally transported wood), and then, not worth the cost of bringing them back, were destroyed. They were destroyed, but not wasted: The larger pieces were used to build other frames, and the rest was used for firewood. Further downstream at Souillac, Beynac, Saint-Cyprien, and Bergerac, solid barges were built out of oakwood. These made the trip several times a year, bringing up wine, salt, and what was referred to as "colonial supplies": lamp oil, rum, and exotic woods to build furniture for the upper-class. The trip downstream was easy. You just followed the current and steered using the rudder and rows, occasionally with the sail. Going upstream, the vessels were towed by the sailors themselves, sometimes assisted by local workers or by oxen.

The people of the river couldn't imagine life in any other way. However, the Dordogne that they loved with passion was not an easy river; perhaps this is why they loved it so much. There are numerous rapids on the trip down, every one potentially fatal. These rapids made upstream travel all the more difficult, particularly since the towpath often had to cross over from one bank to the other. Three rapids in the Lalinde region were particularly feared: the Grand Thoret, the Gratusse, and the Gratussou. They were feared to such an extent that the barge operators themselves yielded the helm to professional pilots to navigate the rapids. Mauzac marks the beginning of the rapids and the first stage of the trip down the Souillagais. Professional

The Tuilières dam at the beginning of the century – juxtaposed with the romantic style of the nearby water ladder.

pilots at the time hired out their services (and rather expensive services, at that). They had a way of making the bargemen realize that without them, well. . . Having guided the barges through the rapids, the pilots left board at Tuilières. From Bergerac on, the going was calmer, with just a few tricky passages. And so went life on the Dordogne River, until 1830, when King Louis-Philippe assumed power and control over navigation projects. It was during his reign that the larger rivers in the southwest were canalized: the Lot, the Tarn, the Baïse, the Dropt, and the Isle. The lateral canal of the Garonne was dug out at the same time. The Dordogne River was equipped with a lock just under Bergerac. To get through the rapids, a canal was planned between Tuilières and Mauzac. The King, however, soon began to worry about the cost of the construction. Alarming news about budgets exceeding their limits were emanating from Lalinde. He one day asked if "these fifteen kilometres weren't going to swallow up all of the Kingdom's gold", that is, the whole of the waterways budget. "It really is the canal of the musketeers, sire," responded a minister, signifying that the project was perhaps more fanciful than serious.

Well, he was mistaken. The Lalinde Canal did have a fanciful touch, but it also had a serious side. In 1840, the three rapids were harnessed by a monumental installation composed of two triple locks. The Dordogne River had become navigable all year round. The professional rapids pilots, deprived of their lucrative monopoly, protested a bit and then became lock-keepers. And that was that. Later, at the

44

beginning of the 20th century, the inhabitants of the valley would thank King Louis-Philippe when an electricity company began using the waterfall to power turbines. The plant, which later became that of Electricity of France, generated light for the whole region. For generations, only one small change has come to alter the installation: the wooden balance-latch doors were replaced by crank-operated metal doors, which still exist today. In the 1950s, barge navigation ceased on the Dordogne. The abandoned vessels reintegrated the ecosystem, the ports silted up, and the dry-dock at Tuilières slowly fell into ruin.

The last bargeman of the Dordogne, Henri Gonthier, is today eighty-eight years old. He recently shared his memories with *Fluvial* magazine (number 75, July 1995). He remembers perfectly how he descended the river with his father on the family barge, the *Jean-Georgette*. They made the trip about fifteen times a year. It took about ten days to get to Bordeaux. In between trips, they repaired and fitted out the vessel. Gonthier relates an exemplary trip dating from around 1920. They loaded the barge in Couze and descended the canal to Tuilières with the help of a cattledriver and his two oxen. They travelled from Tuilières to Bergerac, where other merchandise awaited them on the Salvette Quai. They continued downstream using the oars and, at Sainte-Foy-la-Grande, they unloaded and then reloaded the barge. At the time, the local inland water transporters went from city to city, much as lorries do today. If there wasn't enough water, they would separate the cargo by distributing it onto two or three smaller vessels (the

The last barge at Saint-Capraise has been radically changed, yet still powerfully evokes fluvial history.

FOLLOWING PAGES
The Dordogne River, near Limeuil.

The sharp meanders of this river are called cingles. They can triple the distance travelled by navigators.

regional courpets) which sat higher in shallow water; their barge would have bottomed out. From Saint-Jean-de-Blaignac on, the water was generally deep enough to put everything back on the barge until Bordeaux – that is, if everything went well, which was not always the case. Time and again, they came upon shallows and had to redistribute the loads to lighten the weight, transfer after transfer after transfer. The mascaret tidal bores were a serious problem for bargemen. Tidal bores formed when the ocean tide met up with the on-coming river current, creating a nasty hump of water that could go as far upriver as Castillon or even Sainte-Foy. The navigators mostly preferred to wait at the local inn until the tidal bores passed. After Bergerac, when the coast was clear, our young Gonthier helped his father hoist the mast and open the sail. As the hundred tons of the *Jean-Georgette* sailed up the river, his father told him all about the treacherous channels and tricky whirlpools. In calmer moments, father and son were united in thoughtful silence. Just downstream from Libourne, our bargemen of the Dordogne met up those from the Isle River, on their way to Périgueux. Sometimes, they formed a convoy and travelled down to the sea together. Were they really so different, these Gallo-Roman sailors? At the Ambès headland, they encountered yet another "tribe", that of the Pauillac boatmen, loaded down with casks of wine. Here, they had to wait for the high tide of the Gironde in order to

catch a ride down to Bordeaux. At Bordeaux, they moored alongside the huge sea-going ships to transfer their cargoes of Indonesian rice, American corn, and still-green Brazilian coffee. There was a healthy hubbub on the round-stone quays covered with piles of moorings, merchandise and cattle. Henri Gonthier finishes his tale: "When we unloaded the barge, we all went to the Café du Globe on the Douane (customs) quay. The café also served as a post office for letters and the valley shopkeepers' lists of merchandise to bring back upriver. On the way home, we travelled by sail until we reached Castillon, and then we found cattle drivers who rented out their services and towed us three or four kilometres to the next relay with their teams of oxen. These towers were approved by the Department of Civil Engineering to travel day and night. The last cattlemen, the Monte brothers from Saint-Pierre-d'Heyraud, stopped their activity at about the time that my father equipped the *Jean-Georgette* with a motor." The last remaining barge of the period is the *Merlandou*, which is virtually impossible to miss when you arrive in Saint-Capraise by the secondary route 660. It came out of the Arnouilh naval construction site at Bergerac before the war (although nobody recalls before which war). It was abandoned at Mauzac in the 1980s – the only vessel still intact (or nearly) of the whole of the Dordogne fleet. Yan Laborie, an archflologist of the region who was

The Mauzac dam where the Lalinde Canal beginscreated a nice body of water for nautical activities.

Limeuil.

eager to conserve the history of the river, managed to get the local officials interested in saving the vessel. It was finally patched up, more from sheer good will than from genuine desire. For several years, the *Merlandou* – looking more like a caricature of a galleon than a barge – transported tourists in the meander of the Trémolat. Run ashore in 1991, it was then bought by the commune of Saint-Capraise. Today, it soaks in its basin of stagnant water, no longer of any ethnographic interest, but nice for tourists' photos.

What does the "Musketeer Canal" look like today? When coming from Bergerac, approximately four hundred metres before the Tuilières dam, you see an enormous breach in the rock mass spanned by a bridge leading to the electricity plant. This is the entry of the diversion, which gives access to the first gatehouse. The ramp is paved with large, flat stones that the beasts of labour could easily climb. Continuing on, you arrive at the first lock chamber. There are six in all, separated by a basin which could hold several boats at the same time. These locks scale the rock mass along with a set of noble, green-carpeted terraces. Some of the doors are unhinged. It is a beautiful site, marred only by the electricity cables from the Electricité de France plant. Only the locals know about this beautiful stairway of water. It is at least as beautiful as that of Rogny on the Loing Canal or that of Fontsérannes on the Midi Canal.

In 1996, the first gatehouse became home to an association; while maintaining a human presence at the site, it also furnishes well-prepared information to tourists stopping by the side of the road. You can walk around the romantic remnants and see a plaque made out of enamelled cast-iron stating that "the navigation of the waters is under the full responsibility of the boaters" ; an engraving on a stone parapet in memory of the accident that took the lives of a whole crew; a few pieces of the fitting-out of an ancient barge pulled out of the water by the association during the drought of 1995. It had quietly been rusting for generations.

Next to the second gatehouse, which is also in good shape, is the dry dock where the barges were repaired.

At the top of the rock, about twenty metres high, you can see the panorama of the Lalinde Canal, the tall trees gently filter the special light of the Périgord region. In Saint-Capraise, the basin has been filled up by a landslide and is host to the poor Merlandou barge – a reminder that there used to be a ship-building yard here, that the scent of freshly sawn wood once wafted through the breeze, as did the echoes of hammers and the songs of carpenters. There is even a drawbridge, albeit modest with its single arch. Four kilometres away is Port-de-Couze. Here the canal has been cut by a drained intersection ever since a vehicle of the Tour de France bicycle race missed the humpback bridge, causing a pile-up and several deaths. If we wish to reinstate navigation here one day, the whole intersection would have to be rebuilt. This is food for thought for the mayors, but it is also a source of consternation for the engineers, who rebuilt the bridge way too low for no reason at all. They were simply totally indifferent to what was underneath their construction.

The Tuilières site is kept up like some sort of romantic ruin.

We finish our tour at Lalinde, the little city that gave its name to the ensemble of the waterways. Here is yet another silted-up basin, another symbol of the ambiguous attitude of local officials towards their canal. The basin contains some water (at least it hasn't been converted into a parking lot), and you can walk around it without falling into potholes. There are even a few lampposts. However, the information panel for visitors says absolutely nothing about the site and this incomprehensible body of water, nor about its past use.

After one last lock, you come upon the running water of the Dordogne at Mauzac. It is a wide river with a sailing club at the mouth of the Trémolat meander. An extremely well-marked route directs automobile drivers to a gazebo offering a nice view of the valley. This is the Cingle de Trémolat and the Cingle de Limeuil. You can't miss them. Yet everyone comes away from the gazebo feeling perplexed, for there is no translation of these Périgord regional-language names. How could anyone guess that cingle simply means "meander"?

ROOF OF THE WESTERN WORLD

THE BURGUNDY CANAL

Auxerre is a small territory in the vast region of Burgundy skirted by the A6 motorway. An arrow indicates the direction to Semur-en-Auxois, you take the interchange for Pouilly-en-Auxois, and you're there. Driving down the expressway, you cross through two enormous rows of trees, which most drivers don't even notice. At this exact spot, boats are travelling in the canal beneath you. You are standing on the dividing line of the waters. If two drops fell at your feet, one would go towards the Atlantic Ocean, the other to the Mediterranean Sea. This is what geographers call "the threshold of Burgundy" and what Henri Vincenot referred no less to "the roof of the western world". But Vincenot, like all great story-tellers, had a slight penchant for exaggerations. His stories plunge the reader into a world of barbaric legends where Gauls, Huns, princesses, and fairies peopled the region: an eternal passage point for travellers from far-away Asian lands.

The gate house in Pouilly, in the middle of the Burgundy threshold, was the highest in all of France. Not any more – now it's the Rhine-Danube Canal with its Franconie crossing that holds the record for Europe.

This mythical place is not easily discovered, as is true for almost all of the canals since the flow of traffic and existence of man no longer revolve around them. In the village of Pouilly, there is no signpost or indication of the threshold in question. This surprised even the French president himself, who came with his family to see this historical site. He openly wondered why the state establishment managing the Navigable Waterways of France hadn't bothered to signpost it as he searched vainly among the small streets and fields.

The Burgundy Canal was built to provide a crossing at the highest point of the route between the Saône River and the Yonne River, that is, between Lyon and Paris. This link had preoccupied many a minister since Sully. Diverse itineraries had

Jean-de-Losne, near Dijon, is still a thriving little water city. The barges waiting for their cargo are part of the everyday sights.

already been studied under the reign of Louis XIV. It was fifty leagues as the crow flies to cross the rich lands of Burgundy. But where could they cut the canal? Whole classes of the School of Bridges searched incessantly to find the answer to the puzzle: "How to make the Yonne River, with its abundantly green banks, flow into the placid Saône River through a granite hell." Whatever the course studied, they always ran into the steep rock formation of Semur-en-Auxois. Under Louis XV, the engineers Abeille and Gabriel finally devised a feasible plan which consisted in circumventing Semur and piercing the rock at Pouilly. This plan had the advantage of making it possible to use the two little rivers located on each side of the route, the Brenne and the Armançon. The itinerary was approved by the King's Council: the canal would hook up with the Saône near the little town of Saint-Jean-de-Losne, already a centre of inland water transport and wood floating activities. It would pass through Dijon, pierce the rock at Pouilly, move down through Monbard where De Buffon had forges to operate, brush up with Tonnerre, and then feed into the Yonne River near Joigny.

To each canal, its great man. For the Burgundy Canal, it was Perronnet, then Director of the School of Bridges, architect and artist. It is he who perfected the plans and presented the budget to Louis XVI for approval. The Crown would pay for the Parisian side; the States of Burgundy – the region as we would say today – would pay for the Saône side. The works began in 1784 with the help of the Army, which supplied men to assist the construction companies. The French Revolution froze the calendar, and Napoleon later unfroze it: he needed heavy transport for the Toulon arsenals and planned large-scale import-export via Marseille. He ordered the working force to be increased with war prisoners, as in Brittany. At the time of Waterloo, nothing was finished. The project was continued during the Restoration and completed under King Louis-Philippe in 1837. The hardest part was boring the hole through the Pouilly rock formation, which took a total of six years of hard labour. All said and done, the canal's construction lasted from the reign of Henri IV to that of the last French King. Now that's what you call continuity of State!

We will now follow this itinerary as modern-day navigators. This waterway unveils its charms only to those who travel it. According to the Office of Tourism, Saint-Jean is the "premier river sailing port of France". It is surprising to see so many sparkling white pleasure boats among dark commercial skiffs. It's like being in an authentic grand port with the many foreign flags topping the moored vessels. There are dry-docks for repairs, specialized craftsmen, and a wide variety of accents in the Café de la Marine. Are we really six hundred kilometres from the nearest sea? Even the topography is difficult to comprehend for the visitor as he drives along the route surrounding the basins. It quite resembles the port of Amsterdam, in different proportions of course. It is a huge rectangle of water surrounded by a garland of landing ramps with two islands in the middle. This is a

"water-station", or a dock if you prefer, formed by a natural depression expanded to accommodate large vessels awaiting unloading. In the beginning, huge timber floats of Jura wood coming down from Lyon were stocked here. One helpful local explained:

-"It is linked directly with the Saône by the bottleneck on your left. But watch out, it is narrow and there is a lot of traffic, now that river tourism has become so popular."

-"And the canal?"

-"After the arched bridge, you have another body of water. That's where we moor barges in need of repair, as it is protected from flooding by a lock. The canal only really starts at the end of this basin."

-"Is it far to Dijon?"

-"Thirty kilometres, but there is almost as many locks, so the trip by boat takes at least a day."

Right from the start, the canal reveals its disadvantage: an excessive number

OPPOSITE
The Dijon port is today full of rental boats. It is also an important place for barge-hotels that take passengers on gastronomical or cultural cruises.

NEXT DOUBLE-PAGE
The old hardware store in Pouilly-en-Auxois.

QUINCAILLERIE
FERS - FONTES   DIA

The Auxois landscape along the Burgundy Canal.

of locks. One hundred twenty-nine of them, almost all of which are manual, for two hundred forty-two kilometres. If you make four locks an hour, you would spend sixty hours – not going anywhere, just rising and falling. We soon wonder why there is a motor, we could just as well be towed by horses! An overpowering sense of obsolescence must be reckoned with.

We spent one whole day in the middle of colza and cornfields on a thin ribbon of water. From each lock, you can see the following one. The canal is an ideal machine for time travel. It teaches us that the length of a trip is counted in days, not kilometres, and that a day isn't measured from one certain hour to another, but from sunrise to sunset.

Had we been travelling at the speed of a convoy of boats or even a single barge, the trip would have taken at least two weeks. Travelling at vacation speed (leaving later in the morning and spending whole days in one or another of the pleasant spots along the way) would take twice that long. The 20th century catches up with you just before Dijon. The canal comes right up next to the airport runway, and the boat is just a few metres from the brightly lit 'V's. On some summer days, the fighting planes in training pass, two by two, over your head, splitting the sky like birds of prey before landing, lights ablaze and flaps full-spread. At night, it's quite a spectacle, but if you want a good night's sleep, it's better to go on to the yachting port at Dijon. A long row of plane trees announces the lovely port's garden. We moored in front of a grove of trees near the Gustave Eiffel monument and the obelisk commemorating the first date, in 1837, when two barges met up, one coming from Paris, the other from Lyon. You leave the city travelling along the banks of a lake where windsurfers dot the water and the scent of chocolate wafts through the air. Then comes the Ouche Valley, a very green, winding route with castles perched high on the surrounding hills. The gatehouses have traditional Burgundy-style roofs and poetic, noble names: Marcs d'Or, Crucifix, Creux Suzon. So many names, so many enigmas. The lock-keepers with their local accents have many roles to play. They are veritable

fountains of information: "You have a nice place to spend the night about fifty metres downstream ... Watch out going there, the bank is crumbling ... The local restaurant is closed today. I can recommend the Deux Platanes, my daughter works there. You're the only boat on this reach, but higher up, you'll probably meet up with the *Pacifique II* coming down, the sailor came to buy my lettuce yesterday. Do want some lettuce? I grow it in my garden." Some very nice little areas offer ideal stop-over points with lush green grass, picnic tables or rural inns. We particularly appreciated Velars, La Bussière, Gissey, Vandenesse and Pont d'Ouche, where we were surprised to see the A6 motorway flying over us on the impressively high viaduct. In a few days of river travel, we had totally forgotten civilization and the car. After a long walk at the Châteauneuf castle and a good climb of about ten locks, you arrive on the roof of the western world. At three hundred seventy-eight metres' altitude, this is the highest reach in all of France. From here, it's a straight shot right down to Paris.

NEXT DOUBLE-PAGE
At the foot of Châteauneuf, one of the nicest stopovers of the trip. The countryside is full of white specks, in reality, the famous Charolais cows.

It is a moving moment, indeed. The lock here is called Escommes. It is in the Saône basin, and the lock-keeper informs us we will be the first to pass the tunnel tomorrow morning and inquires as to what time we would like to leave. They will turn on the green light, which ensures that nobody is coming in the opposite direction. From this lock on, it is a one-way route, what is called an "alternating". There is a feeling of well-developed technology and modernity, quite unlike what we have experienced up until now. The Saône basin is an immense man-made stretch of water with a few tufts

A boat below ground level. We are sinking into the trench just before the underground.

of reeds here and there. As night falls, the fishermen fold up their rods and head home on their mopeds. You suddenly feel quite alone, lost among the cries of the lak e birds and the splashing of frogs.

The next morning, as the aroma of coffee and toast waft around the boat, a blue car with the seal Voies Navigables (navigable waterways) pulls up next to us. The driver greets us and then checks that we have all the necessary equipment to confront the perils of the trip: a variety of odds and ends, ranging from a boat hook, a horn, one life-vest per person, enough petrol for the trip, and a searchlight, which he asks us to turn on. We are quite impressed by the organization of the canal, far from imagining the multitude of actors involved in its functioning. We are especially moved by the idea of what lies before us and requires such elaborate precautions. When starting up the motor, we verify the instruments like never before. We idle into a dark and ever-deeper trench, deeper not because we are actually going down, but because the banks are going up. This trench, with its symmetrical walls and stairways, has all the configurations of a Vauban fortress. Before us is a whole set of terraces and low walls marking the entry of the tunnel. We have to turn on the head-lamps and the projector. This is it: we are travelling underground, in a boat, in a vaulted passageway. It takes sharp eyes to see the white point (at a distance of three

thousand three hundred thirty-three metres, according to one map and three thousand three hundred fifty-nine, according to another) which marks the exit. The projector illuminates the very low ceiling and the sides of the passage made out of freestone. We quickly learn to correct the slight orientations of the boat to avoid hitting the walls, which makes a horrible scraping sound amplified by an organ pipe. Travel is extra-slow, on the lowest throttle position, so as not to make waves. At this speed, it takes about one hour to go through. From time to time, we come across ventilation shafts, which furnish rare sources of light. One thought thrill us: the cars travelling at one hundred thirty kilometres per hour above our heads have absoutely no idea what's going on beneath them. We do.

At the exit, there is another curved trench to negociate before reaching a new basin, fully equipped for pleasure boating. On the side of the road, the quay is newly paved, lit, and decorated with flowers. There are sixteen water taps and seventy-eight electrical outlets for the three boats moored here. The developers had big plans for Pouilly.

This port is kept in water by a lock called Yonne 1. The other gates follow suit, going up to Yonne 115. On the bank next to the gate, we see an ancient vessel. It is the old warping tug that used to pull the barges in the tunnel (there was obviously no place for horses). The warping tug pulled whole convoys of barges in shuttles at

Above the sailors, the tunnel is a nice walking path with lots of plants. Not so long ago, the crossing was effectuated with an electric pulley towing the vessel.

fixed hours. In full swing at the beginning of this century, the traffic was thick, with dozens of boats waiting on each side of the tunnel. The local papers gave the tug's time schedule, much as for trains today. The tug was operated by a revolving drum winding a massive chain and then letting it fall behind as the tug moved forward. It was electrically powered, getting the juice from a cable on the ceiling of the tunnel, in tramway style. The electricity to power the tug was produced right there, in a little plant next to the Yonne 1 gate, using the same waterfall. It also served to light up the tunnel and furnish the Department of Civil Engineering's workshop with power to operate its drill and rig. In 1903, it was considered a very modern installation, one of the first applications of industrial electricity in France. It was a source of national pride, and all sorts of delegations, engineering students, and foreign technicians came to visit it. The warping tug service was discontinued in the 1970s after a long and brilliant career.

Before 1903, the tug was steam-powered, the steam escaping through the ventilation shafts. In the very beginning, the barges were pulled by poor peasants who offered their services at the mouth of the tunnel. They pushed the barges along using gaffs and the walls as leverage. At the rate of one metre per push, they sometimes laboured the whole day to get one vessel through. It was a relatively unknown torture that the poor folk endured in silence.

The different styles of art are all mixed together without affecting the harmony of the site. The Viaduct of Oisilly in the Côte-d'Or region.

FOLLOWING DOUBLE-PAGE
The Laumes Plain, where Caesar concentrated his troops to take Alesia. It is today a very peaceful vantage point.

Visiting the Buffon Forges reminds us of the industrious and productive atmosphere of the Enlightenment period.

After having seen the underside of the tunnel, we took the bikes which we had on board and set out to see its upper side. You really have to go to the hollow of the town, on the outskirts of Yonne, to get an idea of the work involved in the construction of the tunnel. The trench was dug with picks and shovels, but the architect, as for most canals, added a monument and a garden. He took incredible care installing all sorts of secondary works, such as pierheads, culverts, stairways, iron parapets, and stoneposts. With a little moss, some solitude and a few fallen leaves, it becomes a park which could have inspired Verlaine. To make the invisible visible, the architect planted four long rows of trees over three thousand three-hundred metres, thus marking the spot. These rows of trees do indeed express the pride of the Department of Public Engineering at having realized an almost impossible task: making it possible for a boat to cross over the threshold of Burgundy, the dream of so many monarchs. It is like a grandiose signature on the horizon, which nearly no one understands (or even notices) in this day and age. The next day, the route was easy and fast, the eleven locks being electric, but the modern world (the motorway runs parallel to the river and slightly above it) seems awfully noisy. If the Eguilly farm-castle is worth a glance, Saint-Thibault, with its strangely disproportioned and mutilated church, is a fascinating site. It used to be a famous place of pilgrimage before a landslide buried it. Continuing on, the boat slowly slides into the Creuzot trench, somewhat worrisome due to its audacious embankments. You then enter a reach about ten kilometres long which leads to Pont-Royal. This is a very nice town for a stop-over. It has been restored to its original state as a mere locality. In the last century, the canal had generated so much activity that it had transformed Pont-Royal into a fairly big agglomeration. There were inns, stables, saddleries, a post office, a canal administration hall, timber floats, a stagecoach stop, and all the other ingredients needed for a thriving business centre. When river transport became obsolete, Pont-Royal went from a booming frontier city to a ghost town. The last inn closed down just a few years ago. The administration hall, (one of the very last in France) now provides lodging for pleasure boaters.

The trip down becomes more difficult from this point on, and we're quite happy to be accompanied by a travelling gatekeeper who prepares each of the locks before our arrival. This is one of the means implemented by canal management to save money on personnel costs. It functions quite well if the traffic is slow. Another method is the self-service gate of which there are only a few. At Frangey, there is also an automatic gate – one among fourteen others – and you can get to Montbard through it. We stopped off at Laumes to visit Alise-Sainte-Reine, an important site in the history of Gaul (the town was then called Alésia), and the adorable medieval city of Flavigny.

We have just crossed the equivalent of a French desert; shops and stores in the area are few and far between. On Monday, food shops and restaurants in France are generally closed, and Burgundy is no exception. This part of the canal has a reputation of being a "sailor-starver". We can honestly say that among the essential equipment of a boat, the most useful item is neither a hook nor a flashlight, but more prosaically, a loaf of bread and a sausage. Behind us is Montbard, a little city where the memory of Buffon still floats in the air. The castle is worth a visit, and the Fontenay Abbey is a must. You can moor next to the N° 69 gate and visit the Buffon forgery, one of the many little factories installed long ago along the waterways. The guide explains the ironworks of the 18th century. This is the most richly touristic part of the trip, and you'll find

The Ancy-le-Franc Castle.

yourself lingering at many spots. The Renaissance castles of Tanlay or Ancy-le-Franc, and the Museum of the Automobile are all in the same area. There are also many curiosities in the town of Tonnerre, homeland of the Knight Eon. You can find out all about these sites since you moor right next to the tourist information centre.

The countryside slowly becomes more and more langourous, the straights longer, the locks rarer. The hardest part is behind us now as we sail due west to hook up with the Yonne. The welcome is a warm one at the Saint-Florentin port, headquarters of a company leasing various types of vessels. Five gates later, you come upon Laroche-Migennes, yet another boat-rental outfit. At Laroche, the canal runs parallel to its "enemy", the railway line, which spreads out impudently in all directions and crushes the night's calm with its bellowing loudspeakers. Obviously, it's a better idea to spend the night at Saint-Florentin. At the far end of the basin is yet another lock, the last one of the Burgundy canal system. It's a double lock, taking you down five and one-half metres and setting you onto the Yonne River. To get to Paris, you go right. We feel somewhat disappointed by the relative banality of the place and the moment. Is this is all there is to the nautical port of Burgundy? Looking around, we only see two perfectly ordinary funnel-shaped banks, more or less grown over. Péronnet is not to blame. According to our hand-drawn plans, the entry to the canal should have been marked by a triumphant Roman-style avenue complete with obelisks. Perhaps francs were running short. The roof of the western world had surely swallowed up the entire budget!

* *Voies Navigable de France* (VNF) is the public body which manages the greatest part of the waterways for the State.

VALLEY OF THE BIZARRE

THE NIVERNAIS CANAL

The Nivernais region – nestled between the Loire and the Seine – is a gentle land of rolling hills, ideal for easy motoring. One nearly fails to notice the steep slope separating Corbigny from Châtillon-en-Bazois. Yet this is one of the strangest sites in all of France.

Far from the paved routes, a deep vale plunges down into the Yonne plain. The tunnel that disappears into the depths of a lake, the multitude of waterfalls, bridges, stairways and well copings all seem mysterious for someone unfamiliar with the world of rivers – all in impeccably cut, moss-covered stones and springing out of the jumbled vegetation.

In autumn days, this is a countryside for poets, and is literally angst-evoking. The thick blanket of fog, the odor of mushrooms, and the obsessive sound of the waterfall will make your blood run cold! In winter, it is a place of absolute solitude. Ice forms everywhere, imprisoning the locks. The stalactite-like sculptures of water and wind form in the run-off pools. There is no sign of civilization. The towpath provides the only access to the canal. In summer, the area does an about-face, becoming a gentle place of wonders. Several of the sixteen locks are entrusted to artists and artisans living in the gatehouses. The small valley literally bursts with colour and life: flowerpots abound, the pig comes when you call, and the geese tug at your trousers, as they do in Walt Disney movies. The locks themselves are painted in gay shades of pink, yellow and mauve.

It's like a little burlesque kingdom. At the second gate, there is a motor on the roof and a half-buried automobile, while a violin

LEFT-HAND PAGE
The Pousseaux bridge rises to let boats pass through.

Homage to the timber floaters of the Nivernais – they provided Paris with its wood supply.

FOLLOWING DOUBLE-PAGE
The Baye Lake constitutes the water storage for the Nivernais Canal. If a boat is coming from the opposite direction, you have to wait your turn near the dike. This is a popular spot with fishermen and wind surfers.

ABOVE
*One of the sixteen Sardy locks,
today transformed into
a pottery workshop.*

stands on top of a post. The laundry drying on a line must not be mistaken for clothing. This is the home of an English artist named Eddie Bonel, who lives amid his creations. Those works for sale are on display in the gatehouse. He arrived from England with a broken-down boat, his young wife and their young infant. The iced-up waters kept them from going any farther. Like explorers of the North Pole, they were prisoners of the ice floe. So, they took root in this part of the world. In summer, Eddie – ever chipper and friendly – is the temporary lock-keeper employed by the county of Nièvre.

Further down, the other lock-keeper-by-chance has converted his house into a small inn. It is extremely rustic and so picturesque that it became a smashing success with the notable people of the region in just a few years. They would come by car along the towpath, which is normally off-limits to all motor traffic. The local police force quickly discovered this gold-mine for issuing tickets, and many a dispute broke out. Although things eventually calmed down, the spell was broken. At last call, the Gros Bouillon Inn had become no more than a drink stand, despite the fact that it was now legally accessible to cars.

In the beginning, the Nivernais Canal was an artificial channel for transporting timber. During the last century, it was converted into a navigation canal for greater efficiency. Supplying rapidly growing Paris had become a national priority. This explains the colossal work accomplished by the Department of Civil Engineering. The ladder, consisting of sixteen locks for three thousand two hundred linear metres of river, was a tremendous undertaking. It had to be cut through virgin forest – all so that barges could descend a total of forty metres. At the bottom, on the Yonne side, Chitry-les-Mines owes its names to the local silver mines, which today have been depleted. Jules Renard was the mayor of Chitry. To the south, on the Loire side, there is a seemingly impassible hill – .impassible, that is, unless someone were to bore through it. This was done, with two tunnels and two trenches into which seventy convicts fell to their death and were buried by a landslide. In order to fill the trench, it was necessary to travel more than twenty kilometres to fetch water and drive it to the site through aqueducts.

The acqueduct of Montreuillon, when viewed from underneath, gives no hint whatsoever that its sky-high pillars are actually ferrying water. The French government must have been well-off at the beginning of the Second Empire: the whole of the works were realized in elegant neoclassical-style flagstone with wrought-iron parapets. This is further confirmed by the discovery that the State also built a bridge over the canal in order to link an isolated farm to the rest of civilization. They virtually built a viaduct for one single household. The farm no longer exists, but the bridge is still there. The boats passed underneath it when they emerged from the second tunnel. It is a true work of art and elegance nestled amongst the abundant ferns – a beautiful and useless monument to the absurd.

The Nivernais Canal begins just south of the Loire, at Decize-Saint-Léger, passes through Clamecy, and then flows into the Yonne River at Auxerre .

Clamecy is the home-town of Claude Tillier, a forgotten name of the mischievous author of *Mon oncle Benjamin* (my uncle Benjamin).

You often meet up with old barges made into hotels on the Nivernais Canal. They make great cabin cruisers.

LEFT-HAND PAGE ABOVE
The Collancelle tunnel in the Corbigny region.

The Lock of the Place in the Châtel-Censoir region.

RIGHT-HAND PAGE
These barge-hotels are the only big boats that navigate here; other commercial traffic has completely disappeared.

It was also home to Romain Rolland, the somewhat less-forgotten author of *Colas Breugnon* ,and to Alain Colas, the sailor lost at sea. Clamecy is also the town of Charles Lecomte, the inventor of timber-floating, or more exactly, the organizer of what you might call the "wood connection" – a highly important part of French history.

Before the industrial era, wood was not only the most important construction material, but also the only fuel used for cars, heating, cooking, and washing. The wood supply was of utmost importance, as is shown by numerous maps dating up to the last war where timber-floating rivers are clearly indicated.

Unfathomable quantities of wood were required in order for Lutetia to become Paris. Many a forest was depleted in the surrounding area, including the forests of Vincennes, Bondy and Sénart. It became necessary to bring wood from farther and farther away, as far away as the old region of Morvan with its hundreds of criss-crossing streams all flowing into the Yonne.

On April 20, 1547, the first timber raft from Morvan arrived in Paris. It was the exploit of Clamecy's master carpenter, Charles Lecomte. A century later, the system was at peak working capacity. The millers had accepted that the waters be blocked by narrows sluices forming reservoirs, and the convents no longer saw them as an offence to religion ... and Parisians were finally guaranteed a constant supply of wood for their chimneys.

In the middle of the 19th century, capitalist concentration weighed heavily in favor of Parisian merchants. They organized themselves into the Compagnie de Paris, headed by a general agent and an elected syndicate which controlled all wood supplies coming into the capital. The Compagnie had a full-scale monopoly and imposed its prices, virtually determining the fate of small communities by its

The Yonne Valley at Mailly-le-Château.

decision whether or not stock wood there. The Compagnie was also responsible for the cleaning of the waterways, fixing the dates for floats, imputing the part of the float costs to each merchant, and so on.

Each year, the floating business provided a million steres of beech- and oakwood to the city of Paris, which represented about ninety per cent of its heating fuel. Obviously, you couldn't just throw a log into the water and fish it out when it reached Paris, three hundred kilometres downstream. It was a highly complex and ingenious system, divided into three phases. The cycle started on All Saints' Day, at Château-Chinon, where the wood fair brought together merchants (contractors), owners (local nobility and clergy), and all other agents of the industry. Sales were made, and all winter long, loggers chopped ten-year-old trees into logs one hundred fourteen centimetres in length.

The logs were branded by hammer with the owner's insignia. This work went on until mid-April. The summer was spent transporting the logs by cart to the river's edge, where they were stacked to dry. In autumn, when the rivers were swollen by the rains held back by dams, the logs were thrown into the water and the sluices opened. Wood covered the surface of the water for kilometres on end. This was le petit flot (the small float). The logs drifted downstream for about thirty kilometres before landing

near a small town which constituted the casting-off port. Here, they were taken out of the water and stacked on the shores. In March, when the rivers reached their maximum flow, the wood was again water-borne and, in a few hours, converged from all sides into the Clamecy reservoir on the Yonne, then came to a rest. This was the big float. The entire surface of the Yonne River was covered with a layer of logs sometimes a metre deep. Clamecy was a major floating centre where the operations preparing the third phase of the process were effectuated. Once again, the wood was pulled from the waist-deep icy waters using a boat-hook. The women and children then sorted it by species, owner and calibre before organizing it into easy-to-count stacks.

The men would then form the logs into timber floats composed of several rafts attached together. Each timber float, seventy to seventy-five metres long and five metres wide, was made up of about two hundred eighty square metres of wood. The rafts were homogenous, supple, and solid, and were able to adapt to the twists and turns and bumps of the journey to come. Constructing a float and putting it into the water was a highly technical operation, carried out by at least six specialized craftsmen. There was a certain way of assembling them with spliced wood. The raft could not fall apart during the trip, and it had to be possible to stop the raft at any given moment. The floater's life literally depended on its sound construction.

The floater navigated the raft standing upright on the shifting logs, and guided the mass with a pole. He rode the current all the way down to Paris. It is not difficult to imagine the risks involved, notably those caused by bridge piles, for example. The floater navigated from sunrise till sundown and moored the raft each night. At Auxerre, they awaited one another to pair up and form crews. The apprentice floaters, boys of fourteen or fifteen years of age, generally left the raft at this time and went home to Clamecy on their own. In his book *Mon oncle Benjamin*, Claude Tillier describes the floater: "Atop of his raft, the water at his feet and the sky at his head, like some sort of insect embarked on a piece of bark, at the mercy of the river. If he strayed a little too far to the left or the right, the raft would break and the man lost his life." (Tillier was probably exaggerating a little bit.)

After about ten days, they arrived in the port of Charenton. Here, the floaters hired a pilot to take the float the rest of the way to the le Louviers or to Grenelle. After which, they gathered up knapsack and lantern and went home on foot – bringing with them the subversive ideas touted by the workers in Paris. Other workers took over from there, and by All Saints' Day, the city-dwellers were burning wood in their chimneys that had been cut two years earlier and brought to them at the price of considerable efforts. This was the wood connection.

In almost all ancient illustrations depicting Paris during this period, you see immense black masses next to wash-sheds and horse-drawn barges: these are the Clamecy timber floats.

In Clamecy, the floaters lived in the Bethlehem parish, a name that undoubtedly came from the Crusades. It was a sort of self-managing republic, nestled between the hills and the river. The inhabitants were big talkers with a touchy sense of honour, to such a point that most thought of them as perpetual rebels. Because of their numerous

travels to the capital, they saw themselves as being a notch above the more sedentary peasants. They had their own jargon and style of clothing and worshipped the cult of Saint Nicolas. They had lots of extremely virile festivities, such as jousting without breast plates or shields. The authorities held them in great suspicion, as is confirmed by the reports of the Prefect Marbière in 1849, describing the quarrels he had with them. He speaks of the bad instincts, hard-heartedness and sarcasms of the floaters. "The slightest rumour, misconstrued administrative measure or the smallest change in their tariffs is enough to start a strike, if not an insurrection." The floaters, belonging neither to the rural world nor to the urban world, were neither of the earth nor the water. They were extremely conscious of their uniqueness. The floater was paid only for his days of effective work (three francs a day for the trip down, nothing for the return). This is why, in their community, they practiced work-sharing and organized a support system for the sick and the widowed. Among the other kinds of rights and advantages, they received the "faix": twenty kilograms of wood per person per day. Sometimes they simply refused to work. For example when the waters were high and you had to get the wood out fast, they got together and demanded a payraise. This is what they called "barring". "You had to either hurry up and accept their demands or thwart their projects by secretly distributing tips and bribes ..."

The Saussois rock formations give you the impression you're navigating in the mountains.

ABOVE
*Saint Nicholas, the patron
saint of all bargemen.*

RIGHT-HAND PAGE
*Auxerre, end of the canal and
beginning of the lively waters
of the Yonne. There is also an
active, colourful pleasure port.*

Timber-floating slowly declined during the second half of the 19th century after the government broke off the Company's monopoly, began to encourage free competition for coal, and favored boat transport for wood coming from the Morvan region. The Nivernais Canal, newly opened, permitted water transport in all seasons, making Parisian supplies much surer. Timber-floating stopped at the Seine dams, but upstream, the free-floating of logs continued up until 1923. It was then that the great torrent broke the Forest Sluice near Clamecy. It was never repaired, and the timber floaters of France simply disappeared. Romain Rolland saw them at the turn of the century. He wrote in his book *Colas Breugnon* : "The wealthy people of the region today will all disappear, but the Clamecy floaters will never be forgotten. They will forever be considered its true nobility – hard-headed and hard-fisted, with their rough hands. And I don't ever want to hear anybody say they were rogues". In Clamecy, you can still see the floaters' sluice, and there is a statue of a floater on the Yonne Bridge, with his high cap and gaff. Flowing right next to it is the canal which contributed to their disappearance. The Nivernais Canal allowed the safe and regular navigation of the margotats, the small barges of the region, which afterwards transported bundles of firewood.

The canal also has the particularity of being county-operated in contrast to most canals, which are State-owned. It was conceded to the Nivernais department, which then assumed the profits and the losses related to it. It came frightfully close to being filled in and was saved only in the nick of time by a pleasure boater in 1960. When Pierre Zivy was blocked there by the lack of water, the lock-keeper told him: "Don't count on any more water than this, they're closing the canal, it's all over." "But I was an acquaintance of the Transports Minister of the time, Marc Jacquet," recounts Zivy. "I went to see him and explained the importance of river tourism in England and how I wanted to start it up in France. The Nivernais Canal, so picturesque with its hand-drawn bridges, was absolutely ideal for this new leisure – especially since industrial river transport had died and ceded the canal to pleasure boaters, who don't bother anybody. He responded that the decree to relegate the canal was awaiting signature in the government, but that he would stop it to examine the case." And so it was that the canal was again placed in the hands of the department and not abandoned. The first boat rental company sprang up in Baye shortly thereafter. At the top of the Sardy ladder, it is admirably well-positioned for those wishing to discover the Valley of the Bizarre.

PARIS-STRASBOURG - MOUNTAIN NAVIGATION

THE MARNE-RHINE CANAL

It first became possible to travel from Paris to Strasbourg by boat in 1853. The trip does take a little patience, but the sights are well worth the trouble. It is a route full of surprises, especially when you reach the hilly region of Alsace, where the boat is higher than the surrounding countryside at times, and lower as it dips into a valley at others – much like a train. Auguste Graeff and Jean-Baptiste Schuilgué, the engineers who designed this water route, were both originally from Sélestat and were graduates of the French Polytechnical School of Civil Engineering.

The first commercial trip from Strasbourg to Paris on the Marne-Rhine Canal was completed by a boat called the *Modèle*. The boat, owned by the Mathiss and Gerhardt Company, unloaded its one hundred thirty-ton cargo at Paris-La-Villette. The trip had taken eighteen days – "at an average speed of five kilometres per hour", wrote the *Courrier du Bas-Rhin* newspaper, "a satisfactory result in terms of anticipated improvement". Along the way, the Modèle had passed the Ulrich Company's *Aigle*, which was headed in the opposite direction and carrying one hundred fifty tons of rice, coffee, sugar and champagne from Paris to Strasbourg. The Paris-Strasbourg link was soon better charted, to the great satisfaction of all: Paris-Nancy required thirteen days, and Nancy-Strasbourg merely three. During this final leg, the boats traveled on the Marne River and were towed by tugs; the first part of the journey was via canals, where boats were pulled by three horses – with three other horses in stables on the vessel as back-up.

The *Modèle*'s arrival in Paris was met with much less enthusiasm then expected. The first link had been completed much earlier, in 1836, by a sailor still famous in

RIGHT-HAND PAGE
At Lutzelbourg, the canal slides down a narrow valley.

Old barge-towing tractors, today abandoned, were very common in northeastern France. They were very cost effective. Commercial vessels like the one on the left have been motorized for years now.

Vitry-le-François is still a major pole for boat works, but has lost the importance it used to have.

Alsace, Jacob Jung. He had made the trip with his two barges, the *Louis Philippe* and the *Neptune*. He travelled along the newly canalized Doubs River, then took a lengthy detour via the Saône River and the Burgundy Canal. The adventure-filled trip was five hundred sixty-four kilometres in all. There was great celebration at the Quai de Bercy when Jung arrived, and newspapers splashed the story in their pages – including his troubles with customs authorities: When Jung explained – in German – that he had come from Strasbourg, the customs officer, who thought that Strasbourg was in Prussia, tried to confiscate his cargo, claiming that it hadn't been covered or sealed as international regulations required. The whole affair wasn't resolved until someone went to the Chamber of Deputies to fetch a deputy from the Lower Rhine.

In 1867, all eyes in Europe were focused on the Marne-Rhine Canal as a smart little steamboat moored at the Iéna Bridge in Paris. A young Hungarian aristocrat named Count Edmond Szechenyi and his crew in full uniform came ashore and explained that they had just arrived from Budapest. He was a thoroughly modern Count, and had come for thoroughly modern reasons: "to open up communication and serve Hungary's enormous industrial development and the growing demand abroad for its products". It was a 19th-century promotional tour! He had built a steam-powered paddle boat

and christened it the *Hableany* (*water nymph*). It was eighteen metres in length, captained by himself, with a crew of four sailors. He had gone up the Danube River before passing on the Main and the Rhine rivers by way of the Ludwig Canal. The Ludwig had just been built by Louis de Bavière on the water-line dividing eastern and western Europe, thus completing a construction site dating back a thousand years to Charlemagne. The most difficult part of the journey was behind the Count once he had arrived in Strasbourg. In Paris, the Count tallied up his exploit: thirty-two days of navigation, one thousand six hundred kilometres and twenty-eight tons of coal. His operation was indeed a success. Not only was he decorated with the French Medal of Honor, but the publicity around it spurred the Dutch and the Germans to launch regular sailing routes to Hungary to buy wheat. (In 1992, the small Ludwig Canal connecting the Rhine and the Danube was re-opened for navigation, and traffic along this route has picked up notably as a result.) The new modern installation, now called the RMD Canal, is very popular among the Dutch and Germans, less so among the French.

ABOVE AND NEXT DOUBLE-PAGE
The access of the Mauvages underground, where barges use the electric towing system is quite sinuous, and one-way only!

Today, the traveller goes upstream on the Marne to Vitry-le-François where the Marne-Rhine Canal

89

*The meeting of a pleasure boat
and a working boat at
Xouaxange and, below,
the boat elevator at Arzviller.
It will first take the big one,
then the little one
(right-hand page).*

actually begins. It is the longest stretch of artificial water in all of France, with its three hundred fourteen kilometres. At Mauvages, the second-deepest underground in France (four hundred to eight hundred metres) plunges you in darkness for about an hour. This is where you pass from the Marne to the Moselle. After visiting a part of the Moselle (although impressive by the large scale of its boats and its modern efficiency, it is not the most charming), you take off to cross the Vosges – the most interesting part of all. Here, the traveller is "filled with awe and respect for the genius who dared undertake this huge enterprise, who amassed masterworks of art and science in this once silent valley". (Frédéric Piton, *Strasbourg illustré*, 1855).

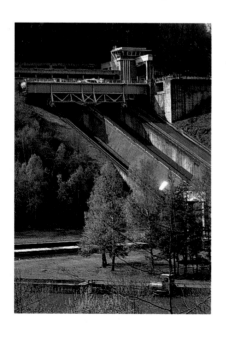

Crossing the Vosges by boat, as those who have had the experience will tell you, is extremely exciting. At Réchicourt, the level difference at the lock is a record sixteen metres, and. it seems like you're plunging down into a well when the gatekeeper opens the lock. In fact, the locks of the Rhône are a little deeper, but they are so long and wide that they make less of an impression. The best part of river tourism begins just after the forest plateau of Nancy, when you reach Gondrexange Lake, a waterfowl reserve. (The waterfowl don't seem particularly bothered by the boats, as they escort you along to beg for food or merely to stare.) Due north, a string of lakes take you to Germany by way of the Houillères Canal – a bit of a misnomer, since Houillères means "coal mines" and the area is a long, green stretch of sheer calm. Due east, you reach Xouaxange, where the canal overlooks the surrounding countryside at an altitude of two hundred sixty-seven metres The boat – now an airplane – quickly converts into a submarine as you are swallowed by a trench-like section that looks no wider than a mousehole. This is the Niderviller underground passage. You quickly reach another passage, the Arzviller, which is the longer of the

two — two thousand three hundred metres of pink sandstone lit with sodium lamps. These two tunnels take you across the summit of the Vosges Mountains. After this, the water flows down into the Alsace Plain by way of the Teigelbach Valley, a modest little vale that nevertheless represents a serious obstacle for a boat. There is a ladder of locks where navigators used to spend the whole day opening and closing the gates of this great stairway of water. Since 1969, however, the boats are lowered in a dizzying elevator built on the waterway — undoubtably one of the last of its kind in terms of sheer scope. This is one of the great moments in river travel.

The works of art mentioned earlier were all decidedly 19th century in style. But now, what we have here is full-fledged contemporary art. We have gone from cast-iron to cement, and the feeling and look of the landscape has changed as a result. Iron, like patterns of black lace, is reminiscent of a Buffet painting. Cement is closer to Matisse. However, the most disquieting thing at this point is what's happening: you're in your boat, your boat is in a huge bathtub, the bathtub is resting on two cable-suspended carriages, and you are being lowered into what appears to be a bottomless ravine — at a forty-one degree angle. Halfway down, you cross two

enormous cement blocks on their way up, and then understand that they are balancing your weight. It takes about twenty minutes from start to finish. When the elevator first came into use, the sailors' wives would frequently abandon ship and descend on foot, leaving their husbands alone at the helm. It was just too much for them. Today, the Artzviller boat elevator is a great tourist attraction, with entry gates, opening hours and, of course, admission fees. Its services are still free of charge for the navigator. It is enormously successful, with two hundred fifty thousand visitors per year. In high season, two ferry boats take on passengers at Lutzelbourg in the sole aim of taking them up, then down, the elevator. And since passenger boats have priority over cargo carriers, the latter sometimes sit waiting for hours until the steady flow of tourists dies down. At times like this, the navigators undoubtedly miss the olden days with their seventeen locks — they were slow but sure. It has been suggested

The elevator has replaced a series of seventeen locks, abandoned but not destroyed.

At the port in Saverne, you can discover an old, restored tractor accompanied by all the explanations concerning the major period of electric barge-towing.

that the old ladder of locks be put into service for pleasure boats. They are still a beautiful sight, abandoned to their solitude for the last thirty years in the midst of fir trees. In such a short time, nature has already begun to swallow up the locks. The astonishing viewpoints are a photographer's paradise and a rich source of inspiration for philosophers. It is a mysterious four-kilometre-long stretch with seventeen locks, an equal number of gatehouses in ruins, and thirty-four rusted doors, most of them askew – all permeated by the odour of leaf mould. In addition to its archflological interest, this route provides fascinating insights into canal-building techniques. Further down, you reach the Savernes lock, a very nice stop-over point which also features one of the rare saving basins. Saving tanks are rare in France: this particular one was built by the Germans in 1880 to replace two traditional locks. The principle behind the basin is as simple, but the movements of the sluices are quite difficult to explain – which is why we won't drown ourselves in details about them here. When the chamber is emptied, part of the water is channelled into a connecting basin, and is then used in the second part of the manoeuvre to fill it up again. It is only partially effective, however, since we haven't yet found a way to make water flow up a grade. Yet a third of the water is saved each time – a precious quantity in any artificial alimentation system.

At the stop-over point across from the Rohan Castle (a sort of mini-Versailles which is spectacularly illuminated at night), there is an old merchant port which

gives you a glimpse of yet another canal technique: a small tractor sits on a narrow towpath with a signpost explaining that in eastern France, convoys of barges were towed by electrical engines along the banks. The system was extremely economical and so silent that no one really noticed when it disappeared in the 1960s.

You know that the end of the Strasbourg leg of the trip is drawing near when you see the Fisherman's Wharf or the Vauban Citadel. You have finished your journey across La Petite France . There is one last surprise: the beautiful half-timbered houses lining the banks just downstream. The Rhine River lies straight ahead. It's a whole other universe. On the right, you see another canal: the Saône-Rhine, which takes you through the valleys of Franche-Comté to the city of Lyon.

ABOVE AND RIGHT-HAND PAGE
The "Petite-France to Strasbourg".

OPPOSITE
The stop-over in Savernes allows you to admire the Rohan Château - lit up at night. This is the grandest port in all of France!

FOLLOWING DOUBLE-PAGE
Arriving at the Fisherman's Wharf in Strasbourg.

THE GRAND MEAULNES REGION

THE SAULDRE CANAL

The Sauldre Canal, which surges out of nowhere and disappears into nowhere, is one of the most moving of the old waterways, and certainly the most forgotten. It was originally built as an imitation of the English canals, and was dug out by citizens on the dole. This canal, another one of Napoleon III's follies, has been sleeping in the mist of the Grand Meaulnes for years now. Who will come to wake it up?

The Sauldre Canal, built during the Impressionist period, looks like it is part of a fairy tale and has provided great inspiration to poets and painters. It does not have the Grande époque magnificence of the Canal du Midi. Nor does it show the technical prowess of the canals in northeastern France. Not a single canal-bridge, multiple lock or monument is found along its forty-seven-kilometre length; it is nothing but a thin ribbon of water nestled in one of the most secret parts of France. It cuts through Blancafort, Argent, and Lamotte-Beuvron, three small towns which exemplify rural France.

Sologne, the name of the region, sounds beautiful when pronounced: it is round in the mouth and gentle, evoking only the sweetest of images. However, in olden times, Sologne was synonymous with poverty and dereliction, as it was haunted by wild inhabitants and was refuge to all sorts of fugitives, rebels, and scoundrels. There were reasons for this, however: the region had no resources, cities or roads, and the only thing that could grew in the spongey landmass characteristic of the region was malaria – incurable for centuries. Neither tax sollicitors nor policemen were ever very enthusiastic about the idea of working in Sologne. Gamekeepers and poachers alike generally met with the same fate: death after a few winters in the

LEFT-HAND PAGE
Lamotte-Beuvron on the tiny Sauldre Canal in the heart of the Sologne region.

region. Since François I, the same theme has come back again and again throughout French history: how to civilize this god-forsaken land by constructing a waterway which would cut through the great curve of the Loire River, somewhere between Briare and Vierzon. The project aimed to improve political, sanitary, and economical conditions. However, plans for the project kept getting lost in the marshes – that is until 1848, when the newly born Second Republic was confronted with the problem of massive unemployment. Luckily, waterways already existed. Fourteen thousand Parisian workers were more or less willingly packed like sardines onto barges headed for Marseille, where they were to take another boat to Algeria in order to colonize it. The remaining unemployed stayed behind to dig the new canal. Cavaignac, a minister at the time, brought out the latest project to date, bought the plans for nineteen thousand francs from its two contented authors, and then went on to modify them. He chose Henri Darcy, an ace of hydraulic engineering, to carry out the plans. Darcy had already provided running water to his hometown of Dijon and had gone on to become Chief Engineer of the Berry Canal. His extremely logical idea was to make the new canal branch off the Berry Canal and follow an itinerary through Selles-sur-Cher, Romorantin, Lamotte-Beuvron, and Châtillon-sur-Loire. That way, it would be integrated into the existing network of navigable waterways and thus be totally efficient. The administration wholeheartedly agreed and insisted that the works start in the middle of the canal, in a village called Puy (or Puet). The government wanted to isolate the "healthy population" of the cities from the anarchists and revolutionaries hired for the construction project. The project got off to a bad start and incidents broke out immediately with property owners in the region. The horse-borne cavalry was called in, and the incidents were quelled. The next year, a plague swept away a great number of labourers, and the cemeteries had to be enlarged to

RIGHT-HAND PAGE
Still in its early days, the canal had to contend with the competition coming from the railways. They actually cross one another at points with bridges. The canal is today abandoned.

make room for greater numbers. What's more, the allotted budget was being surpassed.

As if this were not enough, rivalry between pressure groups and those with commercial interests broke out, under the guise of a technical debate. The canal would improve not only sanitary conditions but also the quality of the region's highly acidic ground soil through the use of marl. A new miracle remedy – lime – was being used more and more frequently, however. And it just turns out that the lime-holders were very friendly with the railroads. So tight was their friendship that the limers insisted on their wares being transported to the region by train. Conclusion: Everything came to a screeching halt.

Then came Napoleon III, who had a few favours to distribute among the dignitaries of his new regime. What better way to fulfil these obligations than to offer a grand hunting domain not far from Paris – providing one didn't catch malaria, that castles could be built, and that the pacified inhabitants made good servants. The solution was, of course, the canal. And so work on the canal resumed, this time on a limited section that did not branch out into the other waterways. The site which had been opened at Puy was abandoned. You can still see the remains of this first attempt near the Motorway 20 and, farther on, along the route from Nouan to Tracy.

In 1869, they began digging the canal at Blancafort – a natural choice seeing

its convenient marl quarries – and continued on to Lamotte-Beuvron, a distance of barely fifty kilometres. It never went any farther. There were twenty-two locks, and the attentive visitor will remark that three of them, those near the Sablière, are not numbered in the usual fashion, but lettered A, B, C. This was a complete anomaly, highlighting the fact that the Sauldre Canal in no way resembles any other of its time. The numbers themselves do not start upstream and go downstream, as was the norm, but begin at the Puit Lake, which feeds all of the canal. This lake of eighty square hectares is today a haven for windsurfers and kayakers – none of whom probably give a second thought to the fact that they wouldn't be there were it not for the canal. The Sauldre Canal undoubtedy killed more people per square kilometre than any other, but it also saved scores of lives. This idea perhaps makes a walk along the banks of the canal somewhat melancholic, even poignant. You simply cannot walk through the misty autumn sunshine that veils this ribbon of immobile silver, rippled only now and then by the fall of an autumn leaf, without thinking of the words of the French author Roger Semet: "On this earth of men, nothing, no nothing, is more beautiful than a canal in October." (Le Temps des Canalous (The Times of the Canal-goers) by Roger Semet. Editions Le caractère en marche.) Game birds and animals abound in the thickly ferned forest and the gunshots of hunters ring out in the distance.

You could say this canal is 100% farming – it has never been used for anything but agriculture and never once for industrial activities.

We had the extraordinary luck of meeting one of the last survivors of the Sologne barge operators shortly before his death. Marcel Bideaut, who had begun working in 1916 at the age of ten, changed professions ten years later, when the canal was abandoned by the government. He used to live in the Coudray gatehouse – which had not yet been equipped with running water by the Brinon locality, despite the fact that its water came from a more than doubtful water table. Was this just another example of the traditional indifference with respect to sanitation? Bideaut recalls that, at the end, there were only four boats in the fleet. Four barge operators (including himself), a chief engineer, four guards who controlled poaching, and seven rangers constituted the whole of this rural society. One would never think to go to dinner at another's house without bringing along a rabbit or a carp. Life was sweet, far away from the modern world and forgotten by the Third Republic.

Up until 1900, the boats were towed by manpower. It took six full days to make the two-way trip. Donkeys and mules were later used, which cut the time by two days. Bideaut recounted this period in great detail. The boats were named The *Terrible*, The *Bayard*, The *Jean Bart*. They were very narrow barges without rudders and were towed by two men or two donkeys, one on each bank. They transported up to sixty tons of marl, firewood, rough timber for the Lamotte sawmill, bricks, and railroad ties. "Ah, but there was one boat that went back into service in '41 or '42," adds Bideaut. "It was used to transport stones to the Route 20. You can note the name, it was The *France* ...."

*The Vieux Peroué
on the Sauldre Canal.*

We saw neither The *France* nor the Grand Meaulnes Castle, so solicited by our imagination. We did, however, see the old brickworks located near the Hangman's Lock, or was it the Mare's Lock? But, do the Hangman's and Mare's locks really exist? You'd think that somebody who wanted to end his life so near a canal would find more convenient means than hanging! The Mare part seems just as doubtful: why a mare? The barges were towed by donkeys and mules, not mares. No, the lock by the brickworks must be named the Gros Castor (Big Beaver), or something like that. The brickworks is just as phantom-like as the rest of the canal. It has everything you need to make bricks – a steam engine, a conveyor belt, carts, and rails, all carefully stocked. We wondered how long the oven had been cold. A day? Sixty years? We pensively closed the door behind us, and were never able to find our way back to it when we tried to visit again.

The canal itself appears perfectly capable of transporting boats. Like the brickworks, Puit Lake, the water station at Jarriers, and the old port at Lamotte-Beuvron, it seems to have been suspended in time by some kind of a spell. I guess in modern-day language, we'd say it's like a frame-freeze – as if a simple electrical contact could put everything back in motion. The canal has not been filled in at all. There are no groves of trees blocking the route, the waterway is intact. Even the locks are in good shape. There is no expressway cutting through it, and the banks of the canal are fairly well-kept thanks to the region's hunters. The gatehouses are still standing, and some are inhabited. They were built in the typical Sologne style with local bricks by an architect who had a flair for style. Their half-moon skylights, semicircular lintel windows, and blue-slate roofs are particularly charming. On the ground floor, each has a common room of nice proportions and a kitchen. Upstairs, there are two bedrooms under the mansard roof. The cellar, which is dry, shows the great quality of the design. A well, bread oven, and garden space complete the house to perfection. In olden times, these homes must have been the envy of many a neighbour, and you realize what a stroke of luck it must have been to get hired by the Civil Engineering Department of the Empire – lodged, heated, practically fed, well-respected and pensioned at that ...

A few of the bridges are too low, a duct needs to be eliminated at Argent, and a few clandestine wells must be done away with here and there, and the countryside would flourish again – all of this just under two hours from only Paris. Oh, Good Fairy of Tourism, where have you hidden your magic wand!

THE LOCKS
OF VERT GALANT

THE BRIARE CANAL

During the summer of 1996, the canal-bridge spanning the Loire River in the town of Briare was inaugurated in grand style. Oddly enough, the bridge had been ready and waiting for over a century. The ceremony was postponed in 1896 until further notice, however, due to fierce local opposition to the bridge. The officials simply gathered up their top hats and their speeches and went home. Briare's residents blamed the new canal for all sorts of woes – the flooding of their cellars and a growing number of destructive animals, among others. And as the constructors were not one hundred per cent certain of the success of their endeavour, they did not insist. Today, however, the town of Briare loves its canal-bridge, so much so that it has posted signs for kilometres around, has adopted it as their emblem, and has even changed the official name of the town to... Briare-le-Canal. In the last century, the Loire River formed a bottleneck on the much-travelled route connecting Ile-de-France and Burgundy. The barge operators had to cross the extremely dangerous part of the Loire between the end of the Briare Canal on the right bank and the beginning of the Centre Canal on the left bank. Between the two, the Loire River churned madly, particularly in winter. A dike over a kilometre in length was built, passing obliquely from one bank to the other. It slowed the current and serves as a walkway. With the help of winches and anchors, travellers braved the elements to cross over. In order to appreciate the difficulty of this exploit, you have to consider that a loaded barge

ABOVE
The Briare Canal-bridge - present and past - on a postcard.

BELOW
The piles support the lamps, which gives a very «Third Republic» touch to the engineer Mazoyer's creation.

113

Palace-style accommodations for the wooden boats.

weighs from two hundred and fifty to three hundred tons, and that it has no means of propulsion. If a barge goes adrift, there is no way to gain control of it again. The barge would be lost, its cargo as well, and perhaps its crew. This crossing was also situated in the direct path of the old fir tubs which were free-floated down the Loire and which were also practically impossible to control. There were often collisions, and many sailors perished each year.

The exact procedure of the crossing has been lost. An ethnological association of the region, which found and restored one of the winches, hasn't yet been able to put together a life-size copy of the equipment – they just don't know the exact order of the operations. They have, however, put forth a reasonable hypthosis, which goes like this: a team of passers followed the barge in another craft and dropped the barge's security anchor upstream. They then carried a mooring down to the destination gate. The pulley-wheels and other components recovered allow us to imagine the way the cables were set up. Once the winch on the bank had seized the long traction cable attached to the barge's nose, the barge was freed to drift into the main current of the river. It could then be winched to keep it in the axis and to guide it to the gate. This operation generally lasted about three hours, sometimes a full day.

The crossing of the Loire was a seasonal operation, which took place during

the short periods when the water was neither too high nor too low. At the beginning of the Third Republic, industrialists in the region lobbied their deputies to modernize the Loire, as the other canals had been. The first among these industrialists was the largest employer of Briare, a mosaic and enamel manufacturer who exported the world over. A canal-bridge in stone, several of which existed in France at the time, was not possible here. The piles would have been too close together to permit the high waters of the Loire, and those of the joining Allier, to pass through. A metallic bridge was then considered; one had been installed fifty years before at Barbirey near Troyes. The problem with a cast-iron canal-bridge was its length. The Loire crossing was nearly seven hundred metres wide at times, and this scared the engineers. It was the development of mild steel, with its weak carbon content resulting in greater flexibility, that finally made the project feasible. The engineer L. A. Mazoyer, then stationed in Nevers, designed the canal-bridge – one of the most famous of all the French waterways. It was made up of two parts: the bed itself, filled with water to carry the boats, and the piles with their stone facings. You have to admire this six-hundred-sixty-two-metre-long steel gutter, which they called the "sheet". It is a trough composed entirely of riveted sheet metal, and although it is one hundred years old, it is still perfectly watertight. From the front, it resembles a large-scale

Pleasure boating above the Loire River.

FOLLOWING DOUBLE-PAGE
There is no more traffic on this part of the Loire.

barge hull: straight edges, slightly rounded angles and a wide walkway on each side. It was a beautiful piece of work, manufactured by the Daydé et Pillé company from Creil (the same company who later repaired it when the army blew it up for no apparent reason in 1941). The masonry was overseen by an outfit famous the world over – the Gustave Eiffel Construction Company. Eiffel really stole the show from the architect Mazoyer: the Briare canal-bridge has always been considered Eiffel's second masterpiece – after the tower, of course.

It was unfair for Mazoyer, however, who was not only an engineer but an artist as well. He aimed to revive the grand siècle tradition in which a canal couldn't be created without a maximum of decorum. He had drawn the four corner pilasters in the shape of obelisks and dressed them with bronze works: Roman-style boat prows, arms of light, and coats-of-arms of Roanne, Nevers, Montargis, and Paris, the cities along the canal route. The sketches are fine little masterpieces in their own right.

Indeed, these Napoleon-style pilasters have permitted the canal-bridge to be compared to the Alexander III Bridge in Paris. They're even better when you consider the strangeness of their context. The bridge in Paris is, after all, one ornamental bridge among many – perfectly in its place near the Grand Palais and the Petit Palais. The bridge-canal of Briare resembles the Alexander III Bridge, is twice as long, and is completely isolated from any other esthetic reference. At night, its fairy-like beauty is astonishing – all lit up (and nowhere to go!) amongst the sleepy shadows of the surrounding countryside.

This fluvial site, the most complex one in all of France, has seen many a modification. Each century, the construction was updated with new waiting basins, short-cuts, willow-lined alleys, or bridges. At one time, there were four gates to descend the Loire. When it became possible for boats to pass day and night – no

The city of Briare has found a new activity with fluvial tourism.

need to wait for the water to rise or fall – the basins became obsolete. The sailors did not miss these paying parking lots. A modern port was dug at the outlet of the bridge-canal to accommodate the growing flow of traffic. All of this gives the modern city not a Venetian, but rather a Dutch feel: pleasure quays and houseboats abound on the street corners and in front of homes. Charming footbridges connect some basins whereas others have been abandoned by all – except for a few ducks and water-lilies.

Navigators simply adore this little city with its water-loop and gracious foot-bridges.

The locks existing before the bridge-canal still exist and are called the Combles on the Briare side, the Mantelots on the Châtillon side. The former is particularly beautiful, a monumental construction in cut stone, where perfectly symmetrical arcades arch gracefully over the rushing Loire.

Once the bridge-canal was in service, the first boat to pass over was the *Aristide*, belonging to a wood merchant from Paris named Guingand. Here, Guingand discovered a marvel of modern river transport in the form of enlarged lock-gates (Freycinet had by then standardized them all to accommodate thirty-eight-metre vessels). On his way to Nemours, Guingand was saved the trouble of travelling upstream through the seven gates of Rogny, the "Henri IV gates". He would have found them much more annoying than impressive: they would have cost him precious time.

119

Rogny-les-Sept-Écluses.

The machinery hasn't changed in its principle.

The seven gates of Rogny – The Locks of Vert Galant – have been conserved as national monuments. They are the oldest-existing locks in France, and provide a very flattering image of the nation's ancestors.

As soon as Sully was appointed "Grand Road-keeper of the Kingdom", (Minister of Transports, in other words), he set out to develop the waterways for the usual economic and political reasons. It was the only way to get heavy loads from the vast Loire Valley, with its multiple riches, to the Seine Basin – equally vast and rich. The Seine Basin was also the point from which Paris, newly reconquered from the Spanish, radiated outwards in all directions. These were not the only considerations motivating Sully (whose true name was Maximilien de Béthune; Sully was a pseudonym he had taken from the town in the Loire where he just happened to possess a castle and a lot of good land).

Leaving Briare, the canal passes by Montargis, the Loing River, and the Seine River at Saint-Mammès. It was to be called the "Canal de Loyre en Seine". In 1604, the engineer Hugues Cosnier took up the construction with six thousand ex-troopers, unemployed since the end of the League wars. The King and his minister "really didn't think it was an insult, but rather a recompense to be employed by this important enterprise". Cosnier was an architect-engineer from the region of Tours who had already worked on the Loire and in Paris. He was a gung-ho boss and led his works in a military fashion. The Loire lock at Briare was drilled at the tiny town of Baraban, on one of the arms of a small river, the Trézée. In 1611, the excavations had reached Montargis when the death of Henri IV and Sully's retirement interrupted the project. Twenty years later, three bourgeois, Jacques Guyon and Guillaume and François Bouteroue proposed to finish the canal. They presented their project to the Cardinal de Richelieu, stating they would finish the canal on condition that they have full usage of it, and went on to form a company with shares, the Compagnie des Seigneurs du canal de Loyre en Seine. They set to work and toiled non-stop. At Montargis, the canal ran through the castle moats which had been enlarged for the occasion. The Loing was, for the most part, canalized in the process. In 1642, the Loire officially became a tributary of the Seine. The first illustrious canal passenger is said to have been Richelieu himself, during his return trip from Perpignan in September.

The canal provided for massive transport of goods from the Loire region, but also from Beaujolais and Languedoc. The merchandise travelling the route was meticulously recorded by the astronomer Lalande in his exhaustive study of the canals at the middle of the next century: coal and hardware from Forez, marble from Burgundy, iron, wood, and faience from the Nivernais region, and paper, fir, coal, and fruits from the Auvergne.

The Compagnie du Canal was a strange mix of feudal domain and modern capitalistic enterprise. The letters patent established it as a fief. The owners took the official title of the Seigneurs of the Canal. They had a castle, a magnificent Louis XIV edifice, today Briare's City Hall. The canal, its peripheral installations, and the lakes and ports all constituted their personal property; they exercised full rights over it all. The entire population pledged their allegiance to the Seigneurs and, in return, were fed, cared for, and protected. The owners rewarded, and they punished. This private justice could go as far as condemnation to penal servitude and even death in the case of murders perpetrated by the personnel. (The High Justice sentences did, however, have to be approved by the provincial High Court). Most of the crimes were related to fish poaching, blasphemy, or pilfering of cargoes. Although the company didn't have the right to mint money, it was authorized to distribute tokens and vouchers in its domain. The owners were most concerned with the moral and physical well-being of their employees, which gave rise to an embryonic form of social security. Riquet was later inspired by this system for the Canal du Midi, which was also set up as a fief. The actual administration of the fief was entrusted to seven or eight shareholders, who met together once a week in Paris. The general collector lived in Paris, and four regional collectors were stationed at Briare, Rogny, Montargis, and Châtillon. The justice headquarters were located in Briare and were composed of a judge-bailiff, a fiscal prosecutor, and a clerk.

For two centuries, the Compagnie wisely managed its holdings in the aim of making them prosper. In 1712, for example, it extended navigation to Buges to hook up with the newly opened Orléans Canal. It also acquired the grant permitting it to operate passenger barges on the Loire from Roanne on up. This made for a nice profit with the growing affluence of passenger traffic. The Compagnie bought houses and forests and constructed docks. It did, however, quickly abandon the direct exploitation of shipping fleets. In the 18th century, independent barge operators could cross the territory; the Compagnie was satisfied with merely collecting usage fees. Briare went from a modest hamlet to a township to a small city. General stores sprang up on both sides of the canal. The docks, still in existence, were dug out and enlarged, each specially designed for its cargo of wine, wood, or pottery. In 1850, a button manufacturer named Félix Bapterosses installed an enamel factory here. It became to Briare what Michelin Tires is to Clermont-Ferrand.

Although the costs of the Loyre en Seine Canal were recouped in twenty years, whether or not it later became a gold mine or a black hole is unknown. The Compagnie voluntarily broke up in 1860 after a long period of decline when everything went wrong. The canal and its management slowly became anachronistic, and nationalism began to surface. The State bought it back, modernized it, and appointed government workers to run it. Briare then became a small naval capital, an intersection of various waterways where Loire River bargemen rubbed shoulders with the canalous (tug-boat operators), giving rise to the expected conflicts. Fights between the two were a common-day occurrence, as both were reputed to be hot-headed types. The street that is today called Cruveiller was, during the canal's peak period, lined with the small local businesses that sailors are so fond of.

NEXT DOUBLE-PAGE
It was here, at the Mantelots de Châtillon lock, that the sailors left the canal to begin the crossing of the Loire, so dangerous in high waters.

STAR OF THE CENTRE

THE BERRY CANAL

There are two villages in France that claim to be the exact geographical centre of the country. Jules Romains would surely have sent them both packing. He maintained that the centre of France was the round city hall building of Ambert in the Puy-de-Dôme region – as anybody who's read *Les Copains* will tell you. All of these self-proclaimed centres are quite amusing to the real connoisseurs – they know exactly where the truly central centre of France is located: it's in Fontblisse! Now, Fontblisse is not a commune, it's just a locality in the land registers, which doesn't seem to bother anybody. It is not easy to find – an advantage since the centre of France couldn't be more than a point, and an abstract point at that. Just like the North or the South Pole, it is simply a precise spot where latitude and longitude intersect in the middle of nowhere.

Such a great place has to remain a secret and mustn't be too easy for just anybody to find: only those with a minimum of perspicacity should be able to access it. Fontblisse is the star of the Berry Canal, the geometric centre of the canals of France. It is a star with three points: one heading west, towards Nantes, another towards the east to Paris and the third and shortest, south to Montluçon. After having wandered around on a lot of one-way roads and followed the vague directions of the villagers, you finally come upon a gatehouse covered in ivy and a dilapidated lock-gate. The mooring posts there are all full of grooves from the years and years of use. This is it: no monument, no stela, no stone post to mark the spot. The three arms of the star radiate out towards their destinations, escorted by the usual rows of poplar trees. There's not much to see here, just three birds

LEFT-HAND AND FOLLOWING DOUBLE-PAGE
An embanked ditch – this is the Berry Canal near Fontblisse.

and two fishermen. How could anyone imagine that Fontblisse was the passing point for thousands of boats (eight thousand in 1912 at the height of activity) on their way to almost every region in France?

The Berry Canal owes its very existence to the French Revolution. The Count of Artois, who later became Charles X, had spent twenty years in exile in England, where he discovered the first industrial canals – a whole network of narrow waterways which were the private property of mines and factories. They were extremely narrow and sufficed to fulfill their very precise roles. When Artois became the King's brother in 1815, he decided that this kind of narrow waterway could be used to cut the Loire River between Tours and Nevers - an area with very bad roads. Of course, being a shareholder in the Vierzon forges, he was thinking of his own private interests and material gains more than those of the people. Cutting this canal would permit him to sell his iron to all the arsenals of France. So he imposed the small-scale canal design, which permitted him to build it faster and cheaper. He didn't stop to consider that upstream and downstream there already existed much bigger vessels: longer and twice as wide. The term flutes, which later became the official name, perfectly describes the design of these slim craft. They are so long and narrow that their proportions are quite similar to those of a cigarette: 28 x 2.60 metres.

The canal was progressively opened to business starting in 1830. The western arm, one hundred forty-two kilometres long hooked up with the Cher River in Noyers after having passed through Bourges. To the south, seventy kilometres of canal to Montluçon. The eastern arm was fifty kilometres in length and joined the Loire River at Marseilles-lès-Aubigny. It was a smashing success. The iron industry of Montluçon and Vierzon, the coal plant in Commentry and the ceramic and glass

works of the centre would never have been able to diffuse their production throughout France were it not for the Berry Canal. The cost of transport was extremely low and soon there were new factories springing up all along the waterways, some of which grew to become powerful industrials. The metal construction plant in Saint-Amand-Montrond and the cement plant in Marseilles are just a couple of examples. All this spread out across the country at the slow, steady pace of the men towing the flutes.

The first vessels were constructed by the carpenters of the Loire boatworks which then multiplied into a string of small sites up and down the waterway. The most important centre of production was Vierzon where more than a hundred craftsmen worked full time during the last century. They built vessels which were called "duck bills" due to their wide, flat front. They were made of oak and fir, their sides were constituted of planks which overlapped like roofing tiles, in the Nordic tradition. They were held together with big bolts and were water-tight thanks to moss stuffed into all the interstices. A duck bill weighed about sixteen tons empty and could carry fifty to sixty tons of merchandise. This is quite a feat when you consider that they didn't sit more than

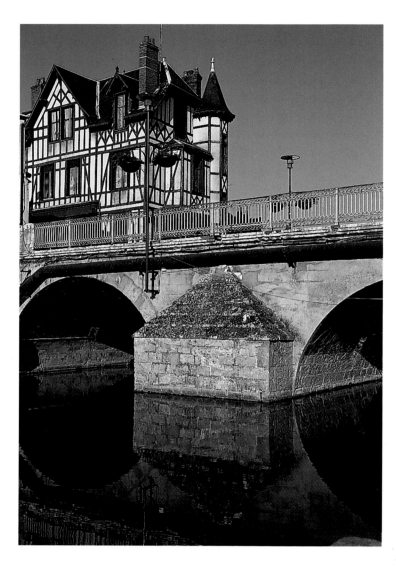

The canal turned Vierzon into an industrial city. Today, the city is restoring the canal and hooking it up to the Cher, for touristic activity.

1.10 metres deep in the water. The duck bills were towed by two men, one on each bank, at the speed of one thousand two hundred to one thousand five hundred metres per hour. This manpower towing was not the living hell that modern stories based on the "black legends" of the 19th century would have us believe. On the contrary, there exist many documents depicting the towers walking at their own pace and shouting jokes from one bank to the other. At any rate, it couldn't have been any worse than the usual labour in the country. The ambition of all salaried towers was to buy a boat of their own and to tow it themselves. Right up until 1914, when human towers disappeared, there was also a rapid service that operated night and day. Rapid travel was the equivalent of thirty to thirty-five kilometres in twenty-four hours!

The conquest of Algeria brought about an enormous change in the life of the canal thanks to the arrival of the donkey! These little donkeys from North Africa could be set up in a stable on board whereas a horse would take up way too much space. As a result, it became possible to exploit the barges in a whole new way; couples did this by living and working on board. The woman led the donkey along the banks.

When the donkey was sick, the woman replaced it ... The man stayed on board, at the helm. Their dwelling was a few square metres in the back of the boat set up as living quarters. How many children were born in these dark, humid cubicles – children who later became hard-working sailors in their own right?

At the end of the century, the flute replaced the duck-bill vessel. It was a more solid craft, with higher sides. Once it was out of its particularly small canal, it had to compete with much bigger barges and carry much more. The flute could transport about a hundred tons. The flat front disappeared and was replaced by a straight nose, which increased the volume for cargo. Under the influence of the other boat-builders in the region, the Berry flute became a small-scale barge and was immortalized by the people of the waters as the berrichon. At the beginning of the century, they were made out of iron, and towards 1920 some of them were equipped with motors. It was a means of transportation that was economical and flexible – perfectly adapted to the historical and economic context. It was also a working unit as well as a living unit for families coming from the peasantry and was cheap enough to be bought by them. For a hundred years, the berrichons were a part of daily life in many cities. You could see them at the apple market in Paris, as floating warehouses for all sorts of materials, fish-farms etc... They would be all lined up side by side in water stations,

The Berry canal near Vallon-en-Sully.

SAINT-LÉGER-SUR-DHEUNE
Canal du Centre

ABOVE
Only the little Algerian donkeys could fit into the stables of a berrichon.
BELOW
The Pont Vert lock on the Berry Canal.
RIGHT-HAND PAGE
The people who live along the canal still remember the old flutes.

fulfilling their role in the local country trade scheme. One of the advantages of its smaller capacity: in difficult areas or in the summertime low waters, only the berrichons could keep on going.

The last wooden berrichon was built by a certain Mr. Chasset and launched in 1951 at Dun-sur-Aubois. Chasset closed his naval construction company shortly thereafter. His berrichon is like some sort of coelacanth- it is the last descendant of the Restoration boat. He seemed quite conscious of this, and christened his craft *Le Dernier Dunois* (The Last Dunois). It worked a very short time in the Berry region, as the canal was abandoned by the state shortly thereafter. Its history is recorded in the Navigable Waterways Register and goes like this: bought in the 1960's it became the secondary residence of a Parisian antique dealer. In the 1970's, it was reequipped and motorized for a vacation camp and spent several summers cruising on the Saône. In the 1980's, *The Last Dunois* showed up in the south of France as the pleasure boat of a chemist from Marseille. Then an architect who understood the historical importance of the craft, decided to restore it and place it in the country's heritage. Unfortunately, it was too tall an order for a single man, and he failed to find any

support with public officials. It was then abandoned in the trading port of Dijon, half-way sunk before being burned by the city in 1988.

Although you can't see any more berrichons made out of wood, there are a few of them left in iron, which have been pulled aground and testify of their existence. We can, however, console ourselves over this loss by going to the two museums which have innumerable documents and objects relating to them: one in Reugny near Saint-Armand-Montrond, the other at Dun-sur-Auron near Bourges.

The Berry Canal also had the job of connecting the Canals of Brittany with those to the east which went on to cover all of Europe. It was an indispensable link. Thanks to the Berry Canal, a barge leaving Saint-Malo could go all the way through to Switzerland – a trip that would be an immense pleasure for contemporary sailors. History carries the memory of one amateur, a Parisian industrialist, who left the Ile de la Jatte in a motorized craft, crossed all of France and then went all the way round Brittany, thanks to the Berry Canal. As for Georges Simenon, he left us his story: *Long cours sur les fleuves et les canaux*. It is a magnificent chronicle of canal life. It must have been a strange set-up - he was a nineteen year-old newlywed and had a little five-metre boat with a motor. It was just big enough for his wife, himself and the dog. But what about the suitcases and the maid? He had to get another craft for the rest, which he towed along behind. He describes how, in the evenings the women would set up the tent while he, Simenon, a Remington typewriter in his lap, concocted the little novel he had to send every week to his editor - to pay for the trip! This group must have had quite an effect on the Berry Canal, whose gatekeepers he described as being phlegmatic "characters of a familiar, smiling and ingenious France". His immersion of several months into the world of canals was so wonderful that he said he had to hold himself back from becoming lyrical! It was indeed a source of inspiration for his first novels and several of the Maigret series, notably *L'Ecluse N° 1*, *Le Charretier de la Providence* and *Le Baron de l'Ecluse*.

BELOW
Dun-sur-Auron.

The essential link of the chain was also the weak link in the network: it was simply off-limits for the large canal vessels due to its extreme narrowness and tight curves. This meant it was inaccessible to and missed out on the barges carrying up to three hundred tons and which corresponded at the time to heavy industry. In 1951, in Saint-Amand, only one boat a day passed through. Closing-down was just a question of time. It soon happened with the decrees that left two thousand kilometres of navigable waterways abandoned. Perhaps if ten Simenons had been through the canal and talked about it, it would undoubtedly have been different – and we would be sailing along it today, from Nevers to Tours. At Marseille-lès-Aubigny, where the Berry Canal joined up with the lateral canal at the Loire River, you see dozens of berrichons that were towed up on land and simply burned. You can still see part of the nose of one of them; why it didn't burn isn't known. The nearby boat rentals company has opened a bar in it.

The Berry Canal offers one of the best examples of what happens to a canal when the State abandons it. Taken off the navigable waterways list in 1953, it was given to the various communes along its banks. Each commune had a sliver of the canal. It was cut into a hundred pieces! Not one of the communes saw the canal as the waterway it was, permitting sailors to travel from point A to point B. No, they saw it as a reservoir or an empty space to fill up. Forty years later, the canal is no more than a dotted line on the map. Sometimes it has become a car-park, a tract of houses, a route, a tennis court, a swimming pool ... or nothing at all: just a muddy trench or a marsh. The few gates that are still visible are walled off or falling down. Many of the reaches are spanned by very low bridges. At Jouet, a police station has been built on the canal's bed. At Bourges, a filled-in reach is nothing more than an empty prairie. At Vierzon, the bridges are so low, there is only a meter between them and the "surface" of the canal – a hotel and a supermarket constitute the definitive obstacles. At Vaux, the canal is walled off. At Valon, it has been filled in and at Tranchasse, it's all dried up.

We here cite the old berrichon proverb: the longer you turn a wheel, the closer you get to its starting point. "What goes around, comes around" for English speakers. Aren't we currently reestablishing the water route between the Cher River and Vierzon, and haven't we heard it mentioned that it might be continued onto Bourges? All we need to do is just redo what we've already done and undone ...

A house in Drevant: this is a commune which is particularly interested in its small section of canal. The old towing path is now a promenade with all kinds of posted explanations.

RIGHT-HAND DOUBLE-PAGE
*Marseille-lès-Aubigny.
An earthen levy condemns what's left of the Berry Canal. This is where it used to connect to the lateral canal at the Loire River forming a fluvial crossroads.*

FRESH WATER BRITTANY

THE BRETON CANALS

Brittany is penetrated by the sea to such a degree that it is hard to imagine there being a need (or desire) to develop inland water activities. So, why is this peninsula, which is so markedly indented, canalized? Firstly, inland water transport came into existence before sea-going transport, which for centuries had been limited to small coastal trade. Sea-travel was both dubious and precarious. The Bretons thus preferred their wide, regular rivers – which unfailingly took them to seaports – to the perilous coastline. They therefore built all sorts of inland waterway vessels long before tuna boats and trawlers. The boats that delivered stones to Rennes were called cahotiers (literally jolters, bumpers); those transporting sand, which were slightly smaller (less than twenty metres long), were called gabareaux (little barges). What was the difference between the two? The cahotier had a flat, upward-turned nose, somewhat like a bark, which led some scholars to believe that they were direct descendants of the dug-out pirogues of the Celts. The gabareau, on the other hand, sported a more classic pointed nose. The innovative inhabitants of Redon even invented a special kind of craft in a category all its own. They were called pénettes and travelled in pairs, attached together at their straight rear ends. Like subway cars, they are amphidromous – they travel in both directions. They functioned somewhat like trailer-trucks: one pushed the other, and then the roles were inversed when one was empty and the other loaded. There were also many different varieties of towed barges, which were collectively called kobars.

The kobars were not a particular type of barge; kobar is the Breton word for

LEFT-HAND PAGE
The Rance Canal.

"barge". At the Redon museum, a cabin from one of these barges is on display. The person inside definitely resembles a bargeman, not a sailor. There is an entire Breton tradition of inland water vessels, their birth and death directly influenced by French history. They first appeared under the Restoration, then disappeared in 1970, after transporting the last load of regional sand.

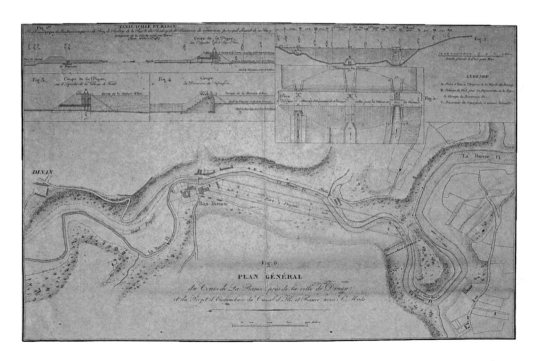

Ironically, the reputation of Breton canals has grown since the disappearance of these vessels, as they don't play a role any more – at least not their original role. The history, which is somewhat complicated, began under Napoleon. Around the year 1800, the English controlled the seabord, and any transport between Saint- Malo and Brest or Nantes was nearly impossible.

Although it was possible to send an inland message by horse, the absence of paved roads made any kind of supply delivery extremely difficult. There were just a few short coastal rivers, more or less fitted out for transport: the Ille, the Rance, the Erdre, and the Blavet, among others. Had they been connected, they would have permitted liaisons from coast to coast. In 1804, an old project designed by the Count François-Joseph de Kersauzon was put into effect. The gigantic construction project, which spanned twenty-eight years, was a godsend for the region, providing employment for the peasants who were jobless in winter. Before irrigating the country, the canal system irrigated the economy. Deserters and absentee soldiers of the Grande Armée were put to work alongside Spanish prisoners of war. They constructed two hundred sixty-six locks, houses, bridges, and overflows in the priority stretch of water connecting the English Channel to the Atlantic coast by way of Saint-Malo, Redon, and Arzal. Three times that number were constructed for the transversal branch of Nantes-Redon-Brest.

During the next century, the Breton inland water system had a lot of ups... and a lot of downs. It was used as an auxiliary for agricultural and industrial activities, but also as an auxiliary for the Navy for transporting ironworks to the arsenals of Brest and Lorient. With time, the downs became more frequent than the ups: Brittany was equipped with roads and railways, and water transport began to seem obsolete. There was a small boom after the war, as cheap transport was needed for reconstruction materials, but an irreversible decline then set in. The State began to neglect the waterways because there were fewer and fewer barges; and there were fewer and fewer barges because the routes were not kept up. In 1922, the State authorized an electricity company to dam the canal between Nantes and Brest near Pontivy in a hamlet called Guerlédan – a blow to the bargemen. This was done to create a waterfall to power turbines. The bargemen of the region had been forced by Colbert to serve in the Royal Marine. When they returned, they found the waterways closing down and the motorways jammed with surplus trucks. The moment was well-chosen to cut the water route to Brest. There had been a few protests, and a lot of cheering from the truckers. It is true that the production of electricity was a priority at the time. The articles and conditions of the electric company's contract stipulated that they had to re-establish the liaison at the first request. However, the requests were never quite adamant enough. (Recently, a minister of the Fifth Republic exempted the Electricité de France Company from honouring this clause

RIGHT-HAND PAGE

Between the two wars, the Guerlédan dam provided the city with electricity. It was cursed by the sailors because it constituted an uncrossable obstacle.

As there are no more bargemen in Brittany, it is today cursed for the same reasons – but by the pleasure boaters!

On the Nantes to Brest stretch.

in its contract.) Today, there remain only fields of mud and decaying wrecks. The ballads of the bargemen are nothing more than a vague memory.

The Breton canals were sinking into oblivion and might have remained there had not a certain René Henno organized several nautical rallies in the region. He was a lover of Breton culture, and his efforts awakened the forest of Brocéliande ... His approach was similar to Napoleon's approach: passing a boat from the English Channel to the Atlantic by inland routes was much safer – especially in winter – than circumnavigating the entire peninsula. Of course, for Henno, it was not the English off the coast that were dangerous, but the tempests. Pleasure boating thus discovered the joys of fresh water navigation, in all its green splendour. The movement really took off in a groundswell of enthusiasm which originated in Brittany and spread to the rest of France. Pleasure boaters could navigate with the whole family and without sea-sickness, in the comfort of boats which were set up like vacation flats and required no permits. The smaller communes attracted a new kind of local-authentic tourism, which was particularly attractive to foreigners. There was no speeding on the waters, no noise, no waves. Inland water navigation is devoid of the mammoth proportions of coastal ports, whose sea wall concessions scare commissioners to death. Inland water navigation is ecological, convivial, and relaxing. It is a form of tourism which includes both nautical and country pleasures, and a return to nature with the prestige of yachting through local tourism, prolonged stays, and cultural and historical discoveries. You are in the garden of France when you are on a canal; it is a sort of backstage landscape which you quietly cruise through. It is the exact opposite of ocean navigation: here, you are literally plunged into the heart of a region, its history, its richness, and its monuments. The canal, in its ensemble, is actually a monument in itself. This is why numerous plans for rehabilitation of the Breton waterways have been put into effect. This has involved over six hundred kilometres of canals where it has been necessary to prune the towpaths, dredge the bottoms, stabilize the banks, and repair the lock gates. It is an enormous job, carried out with the legendary stubbornness of the Armorican people. Brittany is spearheading the movement, with its three ateliers fully devoted to the renovation of the canals. As the work is carried out, flowers are being planted and signs posted, making the Breton canals some of the most beautiful in all of France. The renovation, as brilliant as it is, seems endless: It is being financed by local funds, not by the State. The restauration has given priority to those areas naturally attractive to tourists, and there are still parts of the system which are total wastelands. Coming from Brest, for example, the new service stops at Port-Cahaix. Upstream, the locks are abandoned, the navigator is blocked in his track, and the walker who continues up the towpath does so at his own risk. On the other side, at Pontivy, you see strings of abandoned locks – always a disheartening sight. The departments have formed an institution to manage the works which commands the State agents placed at its disposition and has a substantial annual budget. It exercises continuity in its decisions and financing which, for a large part, explains the success of freshwater navigation in Brittany. What's more, there are no tolls on the canals of Brittany, whereas there are almost everywhere else in France, as the institution managing the waterways wanted it to be free of charge. This is just one more of the advantages of decentralization.

A gate on the Blavet.

ABOVE
From Pontivy to Redon.

BELOW
The Rance canal.

The incomparable ensemble of Breton waterways snakes its way through schist formations, and meanders among broom and ferns before plunging into the sea. It often reaches the coast through deep estuaries in places such as La Roche-Bernard, Lorient, Brest, and Dinan.

It passes through well-known river sites such as Hennebont, Malestroit, Josselin, Redon, Port-Launay, and many others. Yet it also leads to other obscure places that you'd have to hunt for on a map and walk a bit to find. Between Redon and Pontivy, for example, there is Royan. It is a town with no particular attractions apart from a camping ground and a pleasure port. From there, if you motor towards nearby Gueltas and Saint-Gonnery, you can see a typical ladder of locks in Brittany. This is the longest, and undoubtedly the most beautiful, of them all. Located on a hillside in the heart of the Branguily forest, it is a magnificent stairway of water with twenty-three steps. It rises to the sky, quietly, gently. There's not a soul around and between each step, a basin full of reeds regulates the water level and provides a landing strip for aquatic birds. At the top of the ladder, there is a little house – the only one for as far as the eye stretches – which is the home of the Chief Lock-keeper, who reigns over this sleepy little kingdom.

-"Do you see a lot of boats?" we ask.

-"Oh, no, pleasure boaters are in too much of a hurry or they're too lazy. For every step, you have to open the gate, moor the boat, close the gate, open the vents, open the gate, go out and then stop to close it behind you ..."

You can just imagine the old-time bargemen, labouring to heave their wooden barges with a hundred and fifty tons of cargo towed by a percheron horse.

If you count a quarter of an hour per lock, it would take six hours to get through the ladder.

At the top, their reward was arriving at the village of Saint-Guérand. It is a sharing reach situated at an altitude of one hundred twenty-nine metres and fifty-nine centimetres, as the National Forest Service informs us. Just beyond, you "sail" down the other side of the hill, towards Pontivy. There are two ladders this time,

one with nine and the other with twelve locks. Another good half a day, because although you're going downhill, it isn't any faster than going uphill. The water that flows down the two sides of the passage comes all the way from Hilvern through a channel that gathers up all kinds of streams along the way These waters are delivered at the top of the great stairway. At the end of the 1980s, the silted-up channel had to be dredged. The company effectuating the work had to get some very heavy equipment up there in order to do so. Unfortunately, they dug too deep, taking out a forty centimetre-deep layer of clay, which had been keeping the channel watertight for over fifty years. The channel has been leaking ever since. That's why this part of the canal has a lower level (only ninety centimetres) despite the use of electric pumps. It's not really surprising that there aren't too many boats seen in these parts.

The other line of shared waters, between the Channel and the Atlantic, is crossed by the eleven locks of Hédé, which are fed by the waters of the Etang de Boulet. Since 1996, the Canal House has been explaining to visitors that the chain of locks was a technological exploit that defied two generations of hydraulics engineers: it took sixty years to complete! When you leave Redon heading due west, you cross through a place much-loved by all navigators: the Ile aux pies (magpie island). It is a steep slope of granite and sandstone. But it gets even better when you leave the canal and travel up the small, sinuous Aff River towards Gacilly with its little port and old barge terminus. There is first a canal, then a river, then a lake – a succession of reeds, forests, and cliffs in the space of a few kilometres. It is a great pleasure to go from the wild fauna to the touristic fauna of this charming little town. Only inland water navigation permits you to experience this kind of short cut in such an intense way.

FROM ONE SEA
TO THE NEXT

THE CANAL DU MIDI

As you set out from Sète for Toulouse by boat, the trip begins with the crossing of the Bassin de Thau. It's like being on a sort of small sea as you feel the cold North winds blow. After about three hours' travel, a lighthouse adds to this impression. Entering into the canal at Marseillan is a strange experience, as there is no real transition. You wonder if you really are in the Canal du Midi as you navigate through the flat, marshy environment – until you take a turn towards the north and come upon the first lock. The basin is oval in shape, and its form is so

LEFT-HAND PAGE
At Capestang, a nice stop under the plane trees.

unusual that it has become a sort of symbol or logo for the canal. Some say that Pierre-Paul Riquet, the canal's "father", designed the locks in an oval shape in homage to the olives that grow abundantly in the region. Others say the locks are almond-shaped, a reminder of the almond tree which grew in Riquet's garden.

In fact, the first locks Riquet designed were straight. After the second or third lock was hit by a landslide, Riquet decided to use the oval shape, believing that the locks would resist the pressure of the earth better if they were curved. It's as simple as that. Of course, this type of lock was more expensive to build, but the curved shape of the locks has become a trademark for the Canal du Midi. In fact, instead of resembling banal locks, they're closer to the decorative basins in a French-style park. They are perfectly well-matched with the little gatehouses and their lovely romanesque-tiled roofs, and light green and old rose shutters baked by the generous southern sun. A few hundred metres up the Hérault is where the famous round lock called the Agde is located. It bears a deep resemblance to a drawing by Leonardo da Vinci, and accommodates about ten thousand vessels each

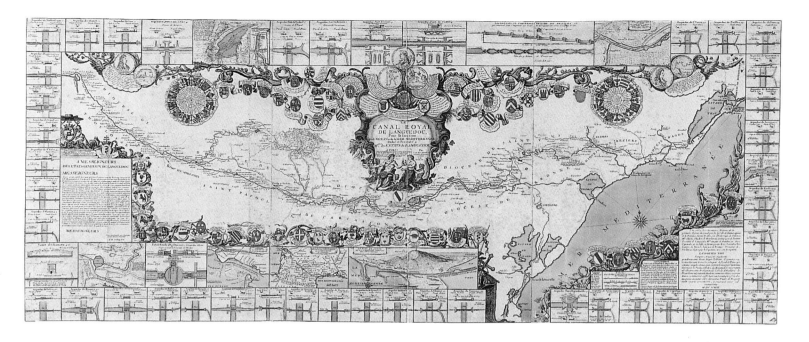

The marvelous archives of the canal show us the ideas and the hesitations of its builders with its watercolour drawings.

BELOW
The round lock of Agde. Engraving from the 18th century.

year. The next interesting spot is the passage du Libron. Although the Libron is a somewhat insignificant stream, it did manage to pose a major technical problem – the Sphinx enigma of waterways. How could the canal and the Libron cross paths without running together? Moreover, how could they remain intact given that the nearby sea is higher in elevation and is pushed by strong winds. The site has seen three different solutions, one each century. The current solution, although not very attractive, has proved the most efficient. In past times, a special boat was floated in the canal to temporarily block it off, letting the stream flow through.

In Béziers, instead of descending into the Orb River – a perilous endeavour in the times of the old barges – we cross over it on a splendid stone canal-bridge. Just after, we start up the Fontsérannes, a ladder of seven locks constituting a veritable masterpiece of monumental hydraulics. Once on top, there is a magnificent panorama of the town and the plain below. As you imagine taking the trip down the other side,

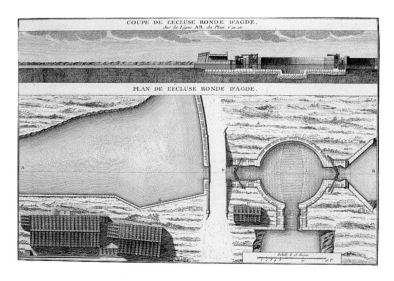

the dread that 17th-century bargemen must have felt becomes nearly palpable. How could anyone imagine bringing a vessel down this steep slope? The seven locks provide an alternative: a crossing device which is an object of great pride for engineers today (when it functions properly). It is referred to as a water slide. With this system, your boat remains in the water and is pushed along the sloping trench by a sort of rolling bridge.

The drilling of Malpas, a great limestone ridge a few kilometres down, is another of

Riquet's follies. The Malpas ridge had a very nasty reputation (dubbed "the bad passage"). Riquet drilled right through the heart of the boulder to let the canal pass through, relying on a rare energy to overcome the obstacles from man and nature he encountered. This was the very first underground canal, and this fascinating site sums up a part of the history of human labour. At the summit of the ridge lies an ancient Iberian city, the archflological site of Ensérune, dating back to the 5th century B.C. Nearby, there are the vestiges of the old Roman road between Narbonne and Béziers. Climbing just before the tunnel, on the north bank, you can see the gleam of the railways built in 1854, which pass underneath Riquet's tunnel. On the other side is a strange circular stretch of land with farm fields radiating out from it: this is the former étang de Montady, drained and cultivated by the monks at the time of Saint-Louis. This is followed by a long reach of fifty kilometres without a single lock. The canal snakes along halfway up the hill. The rocky arid hills on the right-hand side are sometimes planted with vines and punctuated by the black slashes of cypress trees. The plain on the left-hand side, which used to be a malaria-infested swamp before Riquet came along, is now an orchard. When the cold wind clears the atmosphere, you can see the snowcapped Pyrenees Mountains from here. Through the open country and under the umbrella pines lies the entry to the Junction, indicated

Thau Lake.

BELOW

A grand premier for the 17th century: a canal in a tunnel.

by an arched footbridge. The Junction is the beginning of the descent to Narbonne and the sea. For now, we are more interested in the little villages perched on the hillsides, such as Capestang, or by the old halts for the Postal Boats like Somail or Homps, whose wide quays shaded by plane trees are indeed a temptation for pétanque players. Two delicious days of strolling ensued, and the restaurant owners of the area even offered to drive us to their establishments for dinner. Near Carcassonne, swarms of tourists pay homage to its five-star attractions. We travel the canal at towing speed – that of Riquet's day. It requires another day under the plane trees to reach Castelnaudary, whose enormous semicircle of a basin appears at the foot of the city. A great lake shimmering under the sun emerges as you come out of the last lock. And we're off to the Col de Naurouze, where the canal converges with the road and with the railway. An obelisk marks the site's historical status. It's best to moor there and walk up to the collecting basin. This is the actual starting point of the canal. In Riquet's day, this octagonal basin was already steeped in symbolism. The first lock is named Océan, and is now adorned with a long line of plane trees. An arboretum adds to the charm of the place, making you want to stay on a little longer.

There's something in the intensity of the greens or the humidity of the air that suggests you've finally reached the Aquitaine. This becomes a certitude at the Villefranche-de-Lauragais halt. It is a unique place, and the canal irrigates the motorway's rest area. At Toulouse, the city has expanded right down to the water's edge; its suburbs are situated on the banks of its widest bend. The canal then passes through the campus and penetrates into the tightly woven urban fabric of Toulouse. A last watery avenue leads you to the Port de l'Embouchure. At this point, the Garonne River is beneath you and the Canal du Midi flows into the Brienne Canal, an ancient local waterway.

The 17th century was truly one of France's greatest periods. All of the Languedoc region's illustrious minds knew of the project to build a canal between the Mediterranean Sea and the Atlantic Ocean. The project had surfaced time and time again, generation after generation, since the days of the Romans. At one point, it appeared to be as definitively buried as the previous King as "against both public and private interests". One man, a tax collector named Guillaume Riquet, was particularly adamant in his opposition. Riquet's son, Pierre-Paul, having long endured his father's incessant scoffing of this fanciful idea, would later take it upon himself to actually design it. Pierre-Paul had a career in salt tax farming, in other words he collected and paid the salt tax to the Public Treasury. He was not the brilliant financier some describe him as, merely an average bourgeois who worked in Revel at an average provincial level. He had paid dearly for his charge and intended to make good profits from it. For thirty years, he criss-crossed the Languedoc region on horseback accompanied by his clerk. He there collected taxes, but also a mass of observations concerning the region – the terrain, the climate, the miserable routes, and the difficulty for carriages to travel along

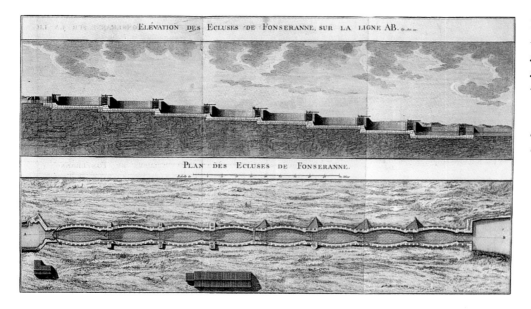

FOLLOWING DOUBLE-PAGE
Nobody can resist the gentleness of a cruise on this green ribbon of water in the shade of its gigantic trees.

The Fontsérannes gates as depicted by an 18th-century blueprint.

A the tip of Onglous, freshwater mixes with saltwater.

them. He became more and more persuaded that the only solution was a canal. When he looked out over the Lauragais and Biterrois valleys, their hilltops planted with vines and rye, he imagined vessels coming through the Gallic isthmus, safe from the Spanish and the English. Riquet then symbolically killed off his father, who had died years before. Yet he himself was sixty years old when officially named adjudicator of the canal works, and would not live to see the project completed.

Carrying off the decision was no light affair. He first presented the project to Colbert, Louis XIV's great minister, cleverly veiling it as a strategic advantage from a modern geopolitical view. What an asset it would be for the kingdom to have a waterway capable of transporting Aquitaine galleys to the Languedoc! A war flotilla – now that was an enchanting idea for Colbert. In all probability, Riquet was secretly thinking more about barges paying canal fees and transporting wine and other lucrative cargo than military strategy. After all, nobody knew the provincial peasants better than he – their needs, their concerns, and their resources.

The Minister was impressed by Riquet, who had one key card in his playing hand: he knew exactly where the sharing point of the canal could be located, and he had years of experience in the field. He had discovered that the waters near Naurouze travelled both towards the Atlantic and the Mediterranean. It was precisely here that

he would place the water collecting reach, thus feeding the canal with the streams running off the Black Mountain. After centuries of projects, Riquet was the first to approach the problem from a realistic point of view. In 1663, the project was admitted by Colbert and his commission of experts. The commission attended a small-scale demonstration of the project in Riquet's garden in Bonrepos. The model rendition of the "Royal Canal of Languedoc" brought the project out of the realm of pipe-dreams and into that of reality.

Riquet studied the Briare Canal, its technique and functioning. He also discovered that the canal was set up as a fief and that its owners were noblemen. They had even acquired handles to their names, along with their feudal privileges. He boarded his carriage with his head held high, a proud look in his eyes. He would be a baron! It was no easy thing to finance the canal. He had all sorts of difficulties: additional clauses to the contract, incessant travels, extra expenses, extraordinary technical problems, and serious quarrels with his engineer, François Andréossy. Riquet was a contractor, not a hydraulic engineer. Neither the ultimate decisions nor the calculations were his to make. It wasn't he who had to act quickly when the substratum proved impossible to work or when the course of the waterway had to be altered. This is so true that we have to wonder if Andréossy isn't the forgotten hero of the

ABOVE
Raisins and water, the perfect couple. Wine transport was, until recently, the reason for this canal's existence.

NEXT DOUBLE-PAGE
The Montady Lake was drained and cultivated by monks 700 years ago. Near Malpas, you can still see the perfect circle of the fields, a curious sight which has nothing to do with the canal.

The Somail Bridge, referred to as being «Roman» is the one of the most beautiful bridges on the navigable waterways. Its clearance is only 3.10 metres, whereas the official minimum is 3.40. Sometimes, sailors have to take down the top parts of their vessels in order to pass under it.

Languedoc Canal. In 1666, Louis XIV signed the long-awaited edict concerning the financing. Seventy-five per cent of the project would be paid for by the Treasury and the States of Languedoc; the remaining twenty-five per cent would be at Riquet's charge. He would receive the finished canal in exchange.

The works began the following year with the collecting of all the streams which would feed the canal. They were united into a "water store", the great Saint-Ferréol basin, where the waters parted paths towards Toulouse and towards Montpellier. At the time, the basin was the largest civil engineering project ever. The tax-collector Riquet, the Baron of Bonrepos, became a sort of general in his twilight years. His army was made up of twelve thousand day labourers, aged from twenty to fifty years and divided into brigades of fifty men. It was not a permanent army, however: in summer, everybody returned home to work the fields. In order to reconstitute his army in the autumn, he often had to overpay the troops. He also paid for sick days and days off. Happy people make good propagandists, and bit by bit the same enterprising spirit spread throughout the valley. When Riquet began work on the Garonne lock downstream, local officials came to pay homage and the prelates blessed the site.

The works went fairly quickly, and the greatest part of the canal was finished in only fourteen years: sixty locks and more than one hundred bridges and works of art for two hundred fifty kilometres of waterways. When it was inaugurated, the canal entered into the realm of marvels of the world. Its contemporaries, such as the Briare Canal or those of Orléans and Givors, would never be able to compete with the Canal du Midi. It went on to inspire a wealth of (fairly insignificant) poetry among poets of the time. It also inspired imitations, in Spain (Aragon and Castille canals), in Germany, and in the American provinces. Statues have been erected in honor of Riquet, and his name is virtually a hallowed one in the south of France. In

1996, his works were hailed as part of the "Worldwide Heritage of Humanity". At the time, everybody who was anybody had to take the Languedoc Canal – from princes to dukes to Thomas Jefferson, then-ambassador of the United States of America. Jefferson, stationed in Paris, took a long trip on the canal in 1787. Being a diplomat (and having a diplomat's budget), he didn't take the Post Barge. He rented a boat and placed his travelling carriage, which he used as an office, aboard. Through him, the Riquet canal undoubtedly inspired the first American canals on the east coast.

The Canal du Midi was much praised for the gentleness of its travelling conditions, the temperate climate, and the sunny disposition of its inhabitants. The trip from Cette (today, Sète) to Bordeaux took six days for a vessel transporting the equivalent of what a hundred carts could carry. The first boats to take the canal were tartanes, small coastal sailboats from the Languedoc region. With time, the tartanes became more squared-off and better-adapted to the shape of the canal. The aim for the transporters was to occupy the space within the lock to the fullest while maintaining enough space in the vessel itself for the handling of goods. In a few generations, the evolution was finished. The lightweight tartane that sailed out of the lock and onto the Etang de Thau had become what was called a master-barge: *Port Somail.*

167

Carcassone didn't want to participate in the building costs when the canal was under construction so Riquet plotted its course further down. A century later, the officials forked out a lot of francs to bring the canal right to their ramparts.

RIGHT-HAND PAGE
The feeder ditch on the threshold of Naurouze is the highest point of the canal.

a thirty-metre-long vessel, rounded off in front and behind, with a rectangular broadside measuring five and two-tenths metres in width. The mast had grown much shorter and was used to attach the towing line and to handle the hogsheads of wine that were being transported. This noble cargo made fortunes for barge operators for years to come. At the end of its evolution, the barge was towed by a horse and carried two hundred twenty tons of merchandise. Other cargoes included oil, salt, bricks, etc. The two hundred fifty kilometres of canal constituted one of the longest inland water routes in terms of travel time, and gave rise to long-courrier boating where the vessel became the permanent living quarters of its owner. The tartanes were indeed built to last. The last of these oakwood giants died of old age in 1982 – after one hundred and thirty years of loyal service !

Passenger transport and postal services relied on much lighter, faster boats towed by two horses. These were the Postal Boats, which had two cabins. Picturesque descriptions from the period give a fair idea of what they were like. On one side, noblemen, bourgeois, officials, ladies and other "persons of quality" sat in a windowed cabin. On the other were commoner's wives with children, soldiers and other "less-respectable" types, straddling various baggages and packets. At best, the Toulouse-Béziers-Sète trip took thirty-six hours. To gain time, the boats didn't use the Fontsérannes locks. Instead, they moored before they reached the ladder, and the travellers crossed on foot where a relay vessel awaited them.

Riquet and his descendants managed their enterprise with benevolent autocracy. All went well as long as all grades – from the lock-keeper to the director – remained respectful and docile. In exchange, they received lifetime employment, an education and a mutual aid system superior to any of those offered by even the most organized corporations at the time. The Riquets were thus able to earn the devotion of whole generations. You entered the canal service by filiation, and this has been the case until just recently. An excellent example is that of the Ramon family. For more than two centuries, the Ramons have operated the cranks of the Canal du Midi. Paul Ramon, the last holder of the title "Lock-keeper of Villepinte" today works at Moissac. His ancestors were Pierre Ramon, lock-keeper at Peyruque from 1777 to 1805 and then at Villepinte from 1806 to 1819; Germain Ramon (Pierre's son) was guardian of the lock and postillion of the Postal Boat from 1806 to 1814, then lock-keeper at Villepinte from 1815 to 1842; Jacques Ramon (Germain's son) was postillion of the Postal Boat from 1839 to 1841 was lock-keeper at Villepinte from 1842 to 1876; Pierre Ramon (Jacques' son) was lock-keeper at Villepinte from 1877 to 1886: Paul Ramon (Pierre's son), Pierre Ramon (Paul's son) and Paul Ramon (Pierre's son) were all employed part-time by the canal; Florence Ramon was lock-keeper from 1958 to 1995; Christian Ramon (Florence's son) was lock-keeper at Naurouze until 1986, then at Moissac from 1989 until today.

LEFT-HAND PAGE
Unlike Carcassone, Castelnaudary immediately took up port activities which extended all along its facades. It has been a washing station for boats since 1964. It is headquarters to the most important boat rental company in France, which belongs to an Englishman.

ABOVE
he ornate letter paper of the **Union des Deux Mers** *(The Union of Two Seas), a boating company that has taken the symbolic dating from the times of Colbert.*

OPPOSITE
The Nègre Lock at Castelnaudary. Watercolour from the18th century.

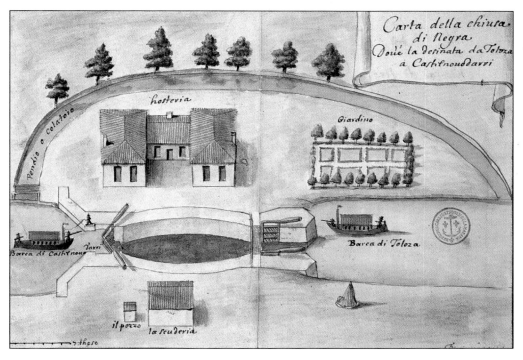

RIGHT-HAND PAGE
*The oval shape is to better
resist water pressure – and not
to symbolize olives or almonds.*

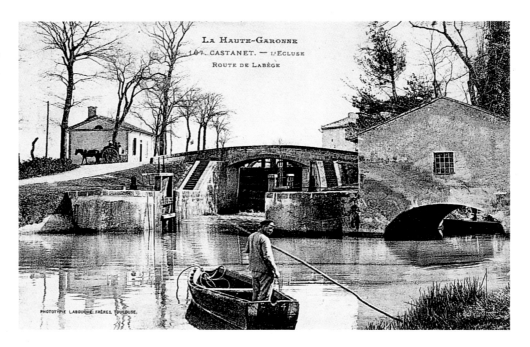

One of the great points of pride of the Seigneurs du Canal was to completely ignore the Civil Engineering School. Their reaction to its creation was to form their own institution – the School of Canal Engineering. It was a fine establishment, given what they worked on: the little Brienne Canal, the Carcassonne derivation, the Robine that descends from Narbonne to the sea. Their works had amazing technical virtuosity (the Libron crossing) and incomparable elegance (the bassin des Ponts Jumeaux in Toulouse).

All of this was accomplished by Riquet's children and the States of Languedoc, who were a powerful group in the 18th century and tried in vain to purchase the canal. In 1848, the State finally succeeded in nationalizing the canal before conceding it to the railway company of southern France, who did absolutely nothing to modernize it, not even when the canal was extended to Bordeaux on one side with the lateral canal joining it to the Garonne and to Marseille on the other side by the Rh™ne Canal. As a result, the canal has not been fully integrated into the network. The locks of the Canal du Midi can receive vessels up to thirty metres in length, whereas thirty-eight-metre vessels arrive at each end of the canal. It's a little like a small country road trying to connect two major motorways. It thus follows that river transport has regularly declined since – except from 1940 to 1945, when private bargemen deprived of fuel went back to using horses to tow their boats. This absurdity obviously did not go unnoticed by the State, who, in 1970, set out to enlarge the locks by the eight metres they were lacking. But, instead of solving the problem, they made it worse: they actually stopped the works halfway through and left the locks non-functional! The Canal du Midi missed out on its chance to become, once again, an efficient transport waterway – all the better perhaps for fluvial tourism, which has made the canal a worldwide success. For some, freezing the canal in its

17th-century state and thus making it a sort of extra-long museum honours the memory of Riquet. For others, it is a supreme insult, in total ignorance of man's unfailing passion for modernization.

Would Riquet have agreed with the engineer Lipsky who, in 1932, wanted to enlarge the canal to giant maritime proportions, four hundred kilometres long and thirteen kilometres deep? Lipsky had a vision of huge sea-going vessels passing from the Atlantic to the Mediterranean through the Canal du Midi. Critics argued that his canal would require five to six times the embankment of the Panama Canal, and would carry five to six times less traffic. Today, the only remains of the project are the inflamed articles that were written about it in the yellowed newspapers of the day: the "sea-to-sea canal" was, and still is, a fanciful myth. The only vessels going sea-to-sea on the canal today are yachts – provided that their keels aren't too deep or their broadsides too wide!

In conclusion, nothing is comparable to this waterway, which initially was so hypothetical that it owes its very existence to a handful of exceptional men, who met at exactly the right moment in French history. Nothing is comparable to the soothing charm of a cruise on this canal, when the plane trees form a roof over your head, gently filtering the hot sun of southern France. Nothing is comparable to the series of magnificent works of art, each one more ingenious than the next, to whom the patina of time has imparted even greater dignity.

Above all, the canal as a whole is the most complete example of the gentle domination of nature by man. Nothing, but nothing in the world of canals, is natural – not a tree, not a drop of water, not a stone got there on its own. We are completely immersed in an artificial environment. It was planned, organized, and mastered by man alone. Riquet and his companions actually loathed nature, which they felt was in direct conflict with man. They were adamantly opposed to disorder and storms, and were strong advocates of knowledge and measure. They re-created this world in their image, seeking serenity and symmetry. Indeed, it is symmetry that welcomes the canal-goers in its double reflection of the world through the mirror-image of the waters. Classical art commanded nature while pretending to obey it. Our period often proclaims itself as obeying nature, all the better to violate it!

LEFT-HAND PAGE
The perfect symmetry of a bridge and its reflection. A bull's-eye for the sailor and his boat.

175

INDEX OF PLACES

INDEX
OF PEOPLE AND CHARACTERS

INDEX OF BOATS AND VESSELS

PHOTOS CREDITS

Photograhs supplied by HOA QUI, Paris, under the direction of MICHEL BUNTZ.

© HOA QUI

T.Perrin : 1, 52, 53, 54, 55, 59, 62, 63, 70, 71, 141 (below)

Ph. Plisson : 6, 17, 140, 141 (above), 142 (above), 144, 145, 146, 147, 148, 149, 150,151, 152-153

Musée de la Batellerie : 7, 23 (below), 89 (below), 113 (above), 142, 172

Musée de la Batellerie, Coll. P. Léger : 37 (below)

P.Stritt : 9, 11, 14, 86, 87, 88, 89, 90-91, 92, 93, 94, 95, 96, 97, 98, 99, 100-101

N. Thibaut : 8, 10, 15, 72, 73, 76, 78, 79, 80-81, 82, 83, 84, 85, 114, 116-117, 118, 119, 121, 122, 123, 124-125, 168

Felix A. : 13, 16, 154, 155, 156, 159, 160-161, 162, 163, 164-165, 166, 170, 174, 175

O.Jardon : 18, 20-21, 22, 23 (above), 24, 25-26, 27 (above), 30, 31, 32 (above), 33, 38, 39,40, 41

G. Guittard : 19, 36, 37 (above a, b), 74-75, 113 (below), 115

M. Renaudeau : 28-29

C. Sappa : 42, 43, 44, 45 (above), 48, 49, 50, 51

C. Vaisse : 46-47

D. Reperant : 15, 56-57, 60-61, 69, 158

De St Ange : 12, 8, 66-67, 68, 134

J. Filter : 102, 103, 104, 105, 106, 107, 108, 109, 110, 111, 126, 127, 128-129, 130,131, 132, 133, 135, 136, 137, 138-139

B. Wojtek : 157

C. Boisvieux : 167

© SCOPE

J. Guillard : 17

J.-L. Barde : 173

© Coll. Simon : 27, 32 (below), 45, 77 (below), 171 (above)

© ALTITUDE

Y. Arthus Bertrand : 34-35, 112

F. Lechenet : 64, 65

© J.-P. Nacivet : 77

© J.-L. Charmet : 171

ACKNOWLEDGEMENTS

With special thanks to the Musée de la Batellerie at Conflans-Sainte-Honorine and also to the splendid team at the magazine *Fluvial* whose staff opened up not only their files and their archives, but also a little their hearts.

Editor
LAURENCE BASSET

Associated Editor
CÉCILE DEGORCE

Art Director
SABINE BÜCHSENSCHÜTZ

Translated by
TAMRA BLANKENSHIP

Photoengraving Graphic Color, Wasquehal, France
Binding AGM, Forges-les-Eaux, France
Printed in France by I.M.E., Baume-les-Dames

Dépôt légal : 2935 – août 1997
ISBN : 2.84277.071.4
34/1233/5